How to Better Serve Racially, Ethnically, and Linguistically Diverse (RELD) Students in Special Education

This important guide offers practical teaching solutions to address the challenges facing RELD students in special education, particularly in high-needs schools where the number of students identified as needing special education exceeds the national average. Written from the perspective of someone with her own lived experience of unique learning needs and marginalization, this book prepares educators to effectively serve our increasingly diverse student population, while also addressing certain special education policy issues and over/underrepresentation of RELD students in special education. Featuring real-life examples and practical strategies to start using in the classroom, this book is key reading for any special educator or school leader striving to ensure special education becomes more equitable and effective.

Buruuj Tunsill is a doctoral candidate at Florida International University. Her research interests include culturally and linguistically diverse students' needs and collaboration with families. Prior to becoming a full-time PhD student, Buruuj taught for five years at an underserved school, where she focused on students with emotional behavioral disorders.

T0373752

How to Better Serve Racially, Ethnically, and Linguistically Diverse (RELD) Students in Special Education

A Guide for Under-resourced Educators and High-needs Schools

Buruuj Tunsill

Routledge
Taylor & Francis Group

NEW YORK AND LONDON

Designed cover image: Shutterstock

First published 2024
by Routledge
605 Third Avenue, New York, NY 10158

and by Routledge
4 Park Square, Milton Park, Abingdon, Oxon, OX14 4RN

Routledge is an imprint of the Taylor & Francis Group, an informa business

ISBN: 978-1-032-64895-8 (hbk)
ISBN: 978-1-032-62739-7 (pbk)
ISBN: 978-1-032-64896-5 (ebk)

DOI: 10.4324/9781032648965

Typeset in Palatino
by SPi Technologies India Pvt Ltd (Straive)

Dedication

Dedicated to all the students I had the pleasure of educating throughout the years.

Contents

Preface

Dissociated from reality, a 5-year-old girl softly places her head on the desk so she can escape into a dream where everything is "perfect." Perfect to her is a happy two-parent household with all her siblings under one roof. The young girl's mom and dad were recently divorced due to persistent emotional and physical abuse.

As a result of dissociation, a couple of years later, the same girl developed articulation issues that persisted throughout elementary school. She was considered a struggling reader and required additional assistance at home and school. Embarrassed by her lack of reading skills, she became even more disconnected from reality. As she grew older, with the assistance of her mother, she improved her reading skills, which in turn boosted her self-confidence and sociability; however, as she became more social, her temperament shifted, leading her down a self-destructive path. Eventually, at the tender age of 18, she found herself admitted in various psychiatric facilities, where she was diagnosed with schizoaffective disorder.

Mental health disorders are not uncommon in the United States. According to the World Health Organization (WHO), mental health conditions account for 16% of the global burden of disease in young people aged 10–19 years of age. Common childhood behavioral disorders include attention deficit hyperactivity disorder, excessive activity and acting without restraint, and conduct disorders. Essentially, childhood behavioral disorders impede adolescents' education. Furthermore, half of all mental health conditions start by the age of 14, but most cases are undetected and untreated. Consequently, unaddressed adolescent mental conditions extend to adulthood, impairing both physical and mental health, which leads to unfulfilling lives for adults.[1]

To delve further into this crisis, in 2020 the National Institute of Mental Health reported that an average of one in every 54 eight-year-old children was identified as having ASD.[2] Impacting more males than females, ADHD has increased in frequency by 42% between the years 2003 and 2011.[3] According to the Centers for Disease Control and Prevention (CDC), approximately 4.5 million children have been diagnosed with a behavior problem, 4.4 million have been diagnosed with anxiety, and 1.9 million have been diagnosed with depression.[4] The issues concerning mental health are persisting, and children are being diagnosed with mental health disorders at an alarming rate. The question is: how do we, as a society, combat this issue?

Eager for answers, the young girl who had been placed in multiple psychiatric facilities for months at a time decided to self-assess so she could not only improve the quality of her life, but so she could help underserved children battling mental health issues. As an educator in a major metropolitan area for five years serving racially, ethnically, and linguistically diverse (RELD) children with emotional behavioral disorders (EBD) at a high-needs school, she witnessed many concerning injustices centered around students in special education.

This book travels through the lenses of an educator who battles with a mental health disorder and touches on better ways to serve students that can help bring some balance to the disproportionality that exists within special education.

Notes

1 (n.d.). *Mental Health of Adolescents*. World Health Organization. https://www.who.int/news-room/fact-sheets/detail/adolescent-mental-health

2 National Institute of Mental Health. (n.d.). *Autism Spectrum Disorder (ASD)*. Mental Health Information. https://www.nimh.nih.gov/health/statistics/autism-spectrum-disorder-asd

3 National Institute of Mental Health. (n.d.). *Attention Deficit/Hyperactivity Disorder (ADHD)*. Mental Health Information. https://www.nimh.nih.gov/health/statistics/attention-deficit-hyperactivity-disorder-adhd

4 Centers for Disease Control and Prevention. (n.d.). *Data and Statistics on Children's Mental Health*. Children Mental Health. https://www.cdc.gov/childrensmentalhealth/data.html

Meet the Author

Buruuj Tunsill is an experienced elementary school teacher with a history of working in the education management industry. She is currently a doctoral candidate at Florida International University, with research interests focused on distance learning; racially, ethnically, and linguistically diverse students' needs, and collaboration with families of students with diverse needs. She is a funded scholar on Project INCLUDE, which is an OSEP 325D project that provides fellowships to qualified doctoral students to better meet the needs of culturally and linguistically diverse students in urban schools.

1

The Purpose of Special Education and Major Cases and Laws that Impact RELD Students

Special education, also referred to as exceptional student education, encompasses 13 disabilities that are defined under the Individuals with Disabilities Education Act (IDEA) as a specific learning disability, other health impairment, autism spectrum disorder, emotional disturbance, speech or language impairment, visual impairment (including blindness), deafness, hearing impairment, deaf-blindness, orthopedic impairment, intellectual disability, traumatic brain injury, and multiple disabilities.[1] The children with a disability under the IDEA law are entitled to a free appropriate public education (FAPE) "regardless of the nature or severity of their disabilities" (U.S. Department of Education). An appropriate education means that the education must be designed to meet each individual child's educational needs, which are determined through appropriate evaluation and placement measures. With an appropriate education, students with disabilities are still required to be educated with students without disabilities to the maximum extent possible.[2]

Hence, public and charter schools are required to provide students with disabilities with necessary supplementary aids and services that will help improve their educational experience.

DOI: 10.4324/9781032648965-1

Gifted education falls under special education personnel duties, but it is not protected under the IDEA. To truly understand special education and what children are up against, it is imperative that each disability is well defined. Racially, ethnically, and linguistically diverse (RELD) students are more likely to be diagnosed with an intellectual disability, emotional disturbance, autism, and/or specific learning disability.[3] Therefore, for the purpose of this book, only high-incidence disabilities will be defined and discussed (i.e., specific learning disabilities, autism spectrum disorders, emotional disturbances, intellectual disabilities, and other health impairments).[4]

Specific Learning Disability

A specific learning disability (SLD) refers to a disorder where one or more of the basic psychological processes involved in understanding and using language—spoken or written—are affected, which may result in issues with the ability to properly listen, speak, think, read, write, spell, or complete mathematical calculations. Conditions include perceptual disabilities, brain injury, minimal brain dysfunction, dyslexia, and developmental aphasia. However, SLD does not include issues that are a result of visual, hearing, or motor disabilities, intellectual disabilities, emotional disturbance, or environmental, cultural, or economic disadvantage.[5]

Autism Spectrum Disorders

Autism Spectrum Disorder (ASD) is a developmental disability that adversely impacts verbal and nonverbal communication and social interactions. Generally, ASD is evident before the child reaches the age of three and adversely affects a child's educational performance. Engagement in repetitive activities, stereotyped movements (i.e., body rocking, head banging, hand waving, or movements that can cause bodily harm), resistance to environmental changes and changes in daily routines, and unusual responses to sensory experiences are characteristics of autism spectrum disorder. Autism spectrum disorder does not apply if the child's educational performance is affected predominantly by an emotional disturbance.

Emotional Disturbance

Emotional disturbance (ED) is a condition that adversely impacts a child's educational performance and displays certain characteristics such as (*a*) an inability to learn that cannot be explained by intellectual, sensory, or health factors, (*b*) an inability to build or maintain satisfactory interpersonal relationships with peers and teachers, (*c*) unsuitable types of behavior or feelings under normal circumstances, (*d*) a general mood of unhappiness or depression, (*e*) the development of physical symptoms or fears associated with personal or school problems. Emotional disturbance includes but is not limited to schizophrenia, anxiety disorders, bipolar disorders, and conduct disorders. The term ED does not apply to children who are maladjusted unless it occurs over a long period of time and is marked to a degree that affects educational performance.[6]

Intellectual Disabilities

An intellectual disability (ID) means below-average intellectual functioning and occurs with deficits in flexible behavior. Intellectual disability manifests during the developmental period and adversely affects a child's educational performance.[7]

Other Health Impairment

Other Health Impairment (OHI) refers to limited strength, vitality, or alertness (including a heightened alertness to environmental stimuli that results in limited alertness to the educational environment). OHI adversely affects the child's educational performance and is due to chronic or acute health problems such as asthma, attention deficit hyperactive disorder (ADHD), diabetes, epilepsy, a heart condition, hemophilia, lead poisoning, leukemia, nephritis, rheumatic fever, sickle cell anemia, and Tourette syndrome.[8]

According to the IDEA, students are entitled to an education that is designed to meet each child's individual needs and is based on "appropriate" evaluation and placement measures. However, evaluation practices have not always been suitable for RELD students.[9] Multiple cases that reached federal courts revealed exactly how discriminatory assessment practices negatively affected RELD children.

In 1971, in the San Francisco Unified School District, Larry P. filed a suit (*Larry P. v. Riles*) claiming that Black students were being disproportionately placed in educable mentally retarded (EMR) (i.e., intellectually disabled) classes compared to the number of Black children in the school system. The district determined students' placement on intelligence quotient (IQ) tests that were racially biased and discriminatory. The court decided (1979) in favor of the students and prohibited the district from using IQ tests to identify or place African American students in EMR classes. In 1984, the court expanded its ruling in the case by prohibiting IQ testing for all African American students referred for special education services.[10]

Likewise, in 1967 Julius Hobson brought a case to the District of Columbia (Washington, D.C.) (*Hobson v. Hansen*) claiming that his daughter was being placed at a disadvantage due to the district's tracking system that unfairly burdened African American students. The court found that the IQ test was standardized to a White, middle-class group, so it was inappropriate to use for tracking decisions; it was deemed discriminatory. This case influenced IDEA-Part B, which called for nondiscriminatory testing and preventing misclassification of special needs students.[11]

Furthermore, in 1970, Diana filed a lawsuit against the California State Board of Education when Spanish-speaking students were administered tests in English, which caused them to be placed in special education classes. At the time, Hispanic students in California were overrepresented in classes for students with ID, making up 26% of students with ID. As a result, California made it a state law that all students should be tested in their native language so that no child would be placed into special education only because of limited English-speaking skills.[12]

As shown above, courts decided multiple cases based on discriminatory practices. Researchers found that IQ tests are an inadequate measure for determining performance on a full cognitive level. Also, evidence suggests that IQ scores are unreliable at predicting variations in performance.[13] IQ tests do not count for creativity, emotional intelligence, and many other facets of an individual. Nonetheless, IQ tests are still used in other states to help determine special education services and placement. When determining whether a child needs special education services, the child must undergo a variety of tests and interact with multiple professionals. The evaluation process is tedious, and it differs from state to state.

In the aforementioned cases, parents filed lawsuits concerning their child's placement. Nevertheless, sometimes there are conflicts during the evaluation process between professionals, where educators disagree with a diagnosis. For example, my sister—a fellow special educator for emotional behavioral disorders (EBD)—met with her individualized education plan (IEP) team to go over her student's assessment results. The eligibility team wanted to give her student an ID diagnosis, but she refused, stating that her student was not ID because he made clever comments and demonstrated academic progress. At the end of the year, the student took a state standardized reading assessment, and he achieved a level 3, considered on grade level. As an educator, you may be placed in situations where you want to remain mute because you feel you are not an expert in a certain area, so you leave it to specific professionals to make final decisions for children they have not seen on a regular basis. As shown in the testimony above, it is imperative for educators to speak up on their students' behalf so they can have the best educational experience. Discriminatory practices in special education occur not only when students are misdiagnosed with ID; it is also an issue in separations, expulsions, and suspensions for behavioral issues due to an ED diagnosis.

As of 2020, approximately 51% of students with ED are RELD students. Additionally, RELD students are 5.47 times more likely to be identified with ED compared to their White peers with disabilities.[14] While identifying students with ED can help improve students' outcomes by granting them the chance to receive special education services, an ED diagnosis for Black students oftentimes results in removal from the general education setting and insufficient learning opportunities.[15] Being educated in a separate classroom explicitly designed for students with varying exceptionalities is suitable for only a small percentage of students. However, data reveal that students from a certain racial and ethnic background are more likely to be taught in a more restrictive environment. Fifty-five percent of White students with varying exceptionalities spend at least 80% of their time in general education classrooms, whereas 33% of Black students with varying exceptionalities spend 80% of their day in general education classrooms. Hispanic and American Indian students with varying exceptionalities are more likely to be taught in segregated educational settings. To further extend, Black, Hispanic, and Indigenous students receive harsher disciplines in school for behaviors.[16] Throughout history, cases have been brought forth concerning students with varying exceptionalities that show a trend of discriminatory practices.

In *Sherry v. New York State Education Department*, a 1979 case, Jean Sherry's daughter, Deloween (14 years old), was legally blind and deaf and suffered from brain damage and an emotional disorder that caused her to self-inflict pain. She was enrolled in a state school for the blind—a residential program—but she was taken out to seek medical treatment for her self-inflicted wounds at a state hospital. While hospitalized, the school wrote a letter to Deloween's mother stating that the school did not have sufficient staff to accommodate her daughter and that her child could not return to the school unless her condition changed or more staff were hired. The superintendent informed Mrs. Sherry that if she attempted to return Deloween to school, the school would suspend her. The district could not provide an alternative program for Deloween and recommended that she go back to the day program until she could return to the residential program.

The mom requested an impartial hearing from the school, and the state school suspended Deloween indefinitely and offered the mom an informal hearing. Later, the school was able to hire supervisory staff, and Deloween was allowed to reenter school. The school's decision to suspend Deloween was determined to be unlawful under the IDEA (then called Education for All Handicapped Children Act).[17]

In the *Honig v. Doe* 1988 case, a student was suspended and later recommended for expulsion because he acted out as a result of his ED diagnosis. The mother felt as the school violated the "stay-put" provision implemented by the IDEA (20 U.S.C. §1415 (j)), which states that the placement in the last agreed-upon Individualized Education Program (IEP) shall remain the same during a dispute and until the dispute has concluded.[18] The court ruled that a student cannot be indefinitely suspended due to disability-related conduct and that the school should continue with the agreed-upon placement until a determination could be made regarding expulsion. The *Honig v. Doe* case is a landmark case that shone light on the "stay-put" clause. However, with the introduction of the Gun Free School Act in 1994, which required schools to implement their own "zero-tolerance policies," RELD students with varying exceptionalities continue to have adverse educational experiences.

Zero-tolerance policies differ from state to state and between districts. For example, in Florida, the zero-tolerance policy states that disciplinary actions should apply to "all students regardless of their economic status, race, or disability," and the policy includes a zero tolerance for battery, which results in bodily injury, but does not include minor fights or disturbances.[19] Jefferson County Public Schools (JCPS) in Louisville, Kentucky, have a zero-tolerance policy on aggression, which includes "fighting, intimidating, threatening, committing terroristic threatening, or harassing students and/or staff; also includes, making bomb threats, vandalizing, and falsely activating a fire alarm." Additionally, JCPS states that schools may "suspend students with varying exceptionalities and cease educational services for a total of up to five consecutive school days in one school year without providing procedural safeguards."[20] Omaha school district in Nebraska has a zero-tolerance policy only for gun violence. The school district utilizes Multi-Tiered Systems of Support for Behaviors (MTSS-B) with hopes of decreasing major disciplinary infractions and improving concentration, positive social behavior, and emotional regulation.[21] Likewise, the Nevada Department of Education utilizes MTSS to help decrease disproportional discipline.[22] Moreover, in Nevada a student with a dis/Ability can be suspended in the same manner as a child without a dis/Ability if the child's behavior does not manifest the child's disability as long as the determination is in accordance with the procedural safeguards (20 U.S.C. § 1415).[23]

Furthermore, the state of Missouri focuses on MTSS and provides positive behavior supports (PBS) to encourage constructive social, emotional, and academic development.[24] On the other hand, the Florence School District in South Carolina implemented a zero-tolerance policy in 2021 that allows educators to expel a student immediately for fighting.[25] Similarly, Texas has strict zero-tolerance policies—although policies vary between districts—that cause many students to be suspended and/or expelled at a disproportionate rate. For example, Houston Independent School District (HISD) has a zero tolerance for behavior that could disrupt instruction or pose safety hazards on school property.[26] States and district policies are constantly evolving; some districts may make serial use of zero-tolerance policies while other districts are more focused on MTSS for discipline. Regardless of the policy, there is still a critical issue concerning Black and Brown students with varying exceptionalities being disciplinarily removed from the classroom.

According to the Office of Special Education Programs (OSEP), in many states—for the 2018–2019 school year—Black students with varying exceptionalities were being disciplinarily removed at a high rate. The data from some of the highest number of disciplinary removals by state read as follows: Kentucky, 251 per 100 Black students; Nebraska, 159 per 100 Black students; Nevada, 115 per 100 Black students; Missouri and South Carolina, 112 per 100 Black students; Texas, 97 per 100 Black students; Delaware, 91 per 100 Black students; North Carolina, 89 per 100 Black students; and Florida, 70 per 100 Black students.[27]

The data reveal that there are disproportionate numbers of Black students facing disciplinary removals.

When students constantly face suspensions, they are more likely to suffer academically, repeat a grade, drop out of school, and become part of the criminal justice system. Moreover, studies revealed that students who are frequently removed from the classroom tend to have lower test scores. These zero-tolerance policies have resulted in a school-to-prison pipeline for RELD students, specifically, Black students.[28] So, what is being done to combat these issues afflicting RELD students with varying exceptionalities?

In 2022, the Office of Special Education and Rehabilitation Services (OSER) and the Office of Civil Rights (OCR) released discipline guidance to help support students with varying exceptionalities and help educators avoid discriminatory use of discipline. OSER and OCR offered positive, proactive approaches to support the needs of students with varying exceptionalities, and they explained the laws related to discipline under the section 504 Rehabilitation Act of 1973.[29] Additionally, in the discipline guidance, OSER mentioned that when using schoolwide approaches and evidence-based programs to meet the needs of all students, schools must implement practices in culturally and linguistically responsive ways that sustain the whole child.[30]

The U.S. Department of Education issuing new guidance concerning discipline and mentioning frameworks (MTSS) that are supposedly being implemented by some states—Nebraska, Nevada, and Missouri—still does not guarantee a decrease of disproportional discipline. However, it is a start in the right direction, and it is up to you, the educator, to implement the valuable information with fidelity. From the inappropriate use of IQ assessments to identify students with ID to harsh zero-tolerance policies, RELD students with varying exceptionalities are being constantly placed at a disadvantage in the education setting, but it does not end there.

A controversial topic, but long overdue for necessary discussions, is state laws concerning involuntary civil commitments and treatment. In 1964, Washington, D.C., established an involuntary civil commitment standard where the person must have an existing mental illness, must pose an impending threat to him/herself or others, or be "gravely disabled" in order to be involuntarily committed to an institution.[31] As a result, states started to implement similar policies that have been adversely impacting Black students. One study reported that all non-White groups were more likely to be involuntary admitted to psychiatric facilities.[32] In Florida, children are involuntary committed every day under the Baker Act (enacted in 1971), and in 2020–2021, more than 38,000 involuntary exams occurred. However, Florida is not the only state involuntarily detaining children; California, Colorado, Connecticut, Virginia, and Wisconsin are also detaining children at higher rates. In Palm Beach County, Florida, several families sued the district for overusing the law, stating that Black children were being involuntarily seized at twice the rate of White children, and it is a disparity that worsens for young children: "40 out of 59 children under age eight examined under the law were Black."[33] Oftentimes, in Palm Beach County, Black children did not receive the benefit of de-escalation strategies and instead, were taken into custody by police officers without parental input. If a child utters any trigger words such as "I want to kill myself," they run a high risk of being committed. Students with varying exceptionalities and/or behavioral issues are subjected to being involuntarily committed at a higher rate.[34]

In theory, involuntary civil commitments seem to be a safe way to protect children, but in actuality, they may cause harm to a child's psyche. According to one study completed on trauma during hospitalization, 69% of participants reported perceived trauma.[35] In Florida, families have reported that children have trouble sleeping after they came home from involuntarily commitment. Also, some students become distrustful of adults, some RELD children who already had fear-inducing interactions with police become even more frightened, and as a result, children and adolescents become silent about their mental health difficulties.[36] A deputy in Hernando County, Florida, stated that typically officers do not contact parents before invoking the Baker Act because they believe parents will show up to the school angry.[37] Children are impulsive and tend to blurt out words they truly do not mean, and who knows a child better than their guardian?

Shouldn't parents and guardians have a say on whether or not their child is taken into a psychiatric institution?

Unfortunately, as an EBD educator, I have experienced one of my students being Baker Acted without my knowledge, and the parents were not informed until after the Baker Act was invoked. The student's dad cried on the phone and was furious that he could not protect his child, and later, I spoke with the mom, who had a similar reaction. I cried with them, as I was devastated for the child; the circumstance also brought to the surface trauma I had experienced from being involuntarily committed as an adolescent. Some may think 72 hours is not that long, but imagine a young child—who has never been away from their parents overnight—being placed into a facility with complete strangers. The trauma that ensues from involuntary commitments is overwhelming. Additionally, trauma impacts learning, which will be explained in subsequent chapters.

Involuntary civil commitments of RELD individuals are an issue across the United States; however, it has been specifically a critical issue for RELD students in Florida. Involuntary civil commitment is yet another law that reveals discriminatory trends toward RELD students with varying exceptionalities. As an educator, you may not be able to change the laws, but you can use caution when implementing laws. Understanding the issues that heavily affect vulnerable groups is one of the first steps to understanding your duties as an educator.

Antonio, a multilingual—Spanish, Creole, and English—fourth-grade student from the Dominican Republic, recently enrolled in Ms. Blaire's class, in the middle of the year. Since kindergarten, he had chronically switched schools because his mother, Nora, couldn't maintain a stable job. Nora has traveled through 13 jobs because she had to frequently call out to support her son, diagnosed with bipolar disorder (Emotional Disturbance) and Other Health Impairment. Unbeknownst to Ms. Blaire, Nora did not want to give her child medication because she felt as if he was not "alive" when he was medicated; he was not himself. Nora believed Antonio's behavioral issues had improved since kindergarten, but that was not apparent to Ms. Blaire. In the first week of attendance, during whole group reading,

Antonio made bird noises and blurted out profanities, which prompted Ms. Blaire to write a referral. During lunch, Antonio walked out of the cafeteria and found a quiet spot outside, by the corner of his classroom. On Ms. Blaire's way to pick her students up from lunch, she discovered Antonio sitting outside and asked him why he left the cafeteria, but he remained mute. In a rush to pick up her students, Ms. Blaire grabbed Antonio's hand and disregarded Antonio's actions, but made a mental note to inform his mom later—as currently his mom had "bigger fish to fry." A few weeks into school, Ms. Blaire witnessed Antonio's short temper when one of his classmates bumped into Antonio in line. Before the student could apologize, Antonio knocked the young boy down and punched him. As a result, he was suspended for five days. Since Antonio had enrolled in Ms. Blaire's class, she became hypervigilant, and her class—as a whole—became more disruptive. At her wit's end, Ms. Blaire vented to the ESE specialist because prior to Antonio's arrival, she had managed to keep her class in splendid order.

While Ms. Blaine was venting to the exceptional student education (ESE) specialist, Antonio's mom walked into the office to request a conference with the teacher. Ms. Blaire overheard Nora speaking, with limited English proficiency, to the front office specialist and intervened to introduce herself and schedule a conference. Ms. Blaire had exchanged texts with Antonio's mom but had never spoken with her over the phone or in person. Although not protocol, Ms. Blaire asked the ESE specialist and support facilitator to sit in with her during the conference to assist her in understanding the parent and to be there in case conflicts arose. During the conference, Ms. Blaire sat with her anecdotal notes to address all of her concerns.

The above-mentioned scenario is a glimpse of the struggles of RELD students with varying exceptionalities and reveals what parents and educators face when working with students with special needs. Now ask yourself, does Ms. Blaire see only Antonio's shortcomings? What could Ms. Blaire do differently to address the issues during reading? Why did Antonio walk out of the cafeteria? In the following lines below, jot down your thoughts.

_____
_____
_____
_____
_____
_____
_____

   The issues that persist for RELD students and all stakehold-ers are troubling, and many questions for educators go unan-swered while other questions continue to surface. There is much to ponder when working with RELD students with varying exceptionalities, and the succeeding chapters will address some of the numerous concerns that surround these students.

Notes

1 Lee, A.M.l. *The 13 disability categories under IDEA*. Understood. https://www.understood.org/en/articles/conditions-covered-under-idea

2 Office of Civil Rights. (n.d.). *Free Appropriate Public Education (FAPE)*. U.S. Department of Education. https://www2.ed.gov/about/offices/list/ocr/frontpage/pro-students/issues/dis-issue03.html#:~:text=The%20%E2%80%9Cappropriate%E2%80%9D%20component%20means%20that%20this%20education%20must,students%20without%20disabilities%20to%20the%20maximum%20extent%20appropriate

3 Office of Special Education Programs. (n.d.). *Office of special education programs releases fast facts on the race and ethnicity of children with disabilities served under IDEA Part B*. U.S. Department of Education. https://sites.ed.gov/osers/2021/08/osep-releases-fast-facts-on-the-race-and-ethnicity-of-children-with-disabilities-served-under-idea-part-b/

4 University of Kansas. (n.d.). *High Incidence Disabilities Definition*. The University of Kansas School of Education and Human Services. https://educationonline.ku.edu/community/high-incidence-disabilities-definition#:~:text="High%2Dincidence"%20disabilities%20may,Specific%20learning%20disabilities

5 University of Kansas. (n.d.). *High Incidence Disabilities Definition*. The University of Kansas School of Education and Human Services. https://educationonline.ku.edu/community/high-incidence-disabilities-definition#:~:text="High%2Dincidence"%20disabilities%20may,Specific%20learning%20disabilities

6 University of Kansas. (n.d.). *High Incidence Disabilities Definition*. The University of Kansas School of Education and Human Services. https://educationonline.ku.edu/community/high-incidence-disabilities-definition#:~:text="High%2Dincidence"%20disabilities%20may,Specific%20learning%20disabilities

   https://www.ksde.org/Portals/0/ECSETS/FactSheets/FactSheet-SpEd-ED.pdf?TSPD_101_R0=0812b43512ab200087a398af3bf8c8684c57790895a8cececd418526f0e97f807fcecfcba62dad29088655262714300017577f28ece5a3a123336c82510f421352d61c204173ab44b94719f737bb62acf4b9ea11cbf6fa2f0d9ab641221fc9ff

7 University of Kansas. (n.d.). *High Incidence Disabilities Definition*. The University of Kansas School of Education and Human Services. https://educationonline.ku.edu/community/high-incidence-disabilities-definition#:~:text="High%2Dincidence"%20disabilities%20may,Specific%20learning%20disabilities

8 University of Kansas. (n.d.). *High Incidence Disabilities Definition*. The University of Kansas School of Education and Human Services. https://educationonline.ku.edu/community/high-incidence-disabilities-definition#:~:text=%E2%80%9CHigh%2Dincidence%E2%80%9D%20disabilities%20may,Specific%20learning%20disabilities

9 Blanchett, W., Klinger, J., & Harry, B. (2009). The intersection of race culture, language, and disability: Implication for urban education. *Urban Education, 44*(4), 389–409. https://doi.org/10.1177/0042085909338686

10 Special Education Rights and Responsibilities. (n.d.). *What is the Larry P. v. Riles case? What impact does the Diana case have on Spanish-speaking students?* Disability Rights California. https://serr.disabilityrightsca.org/serr-manual/chapter-2-information-on-evaluations-assessments/2-45-what-is-the-larry-p-v-riles-case-how-did-it-originate/

11 Mrsledge. (n.d.). *History of Special Education: Important Landmark Cases*. Time Toast. https://www.timetoast.com/timelines/history-of-special-education-important-landmark-cases

12 Special Education Rights and Responsibilities. (n.d.). *What was the Diana v. State Board of Education case? What impact does the Diana case have on Spanish-speaking students?* Disability Rights California. https://serr.disabilityrightsca.org/serr-manual/chapter-2-information-on-evaluations-assessments/2-48-what-was-the-diana-v-state-board-of-education-case-what-impact-does-the-diana-case-have-on-spanish-speaking-students/

13 Ganuthula, V.R.R., & Sinha, S. (2019, December 17). The Looking glass for intelligence quotient tests: The Interplay of motivation, cognitive functioning, and affect. *Frontiers in Psychology, 10*, 2857. https://doi.org/10.3389/fpsyg.2019.02857.
PMID: 31920882; PMCID: PMC6927908.

14 Office of Special Education Programs. (n.d.). *Fast facts on the race and ethnicity of children with disabilities served under IDEA Part B*. U.S. Department of Education. https://sites.ed.gov/idea/osep-fast-facts-race-and-ethnicity-of-children-with-disabilities-served-under-idea-part-b/

15 Office of Special Education Programs (n.d.). *Office of special education programs releases fast facts on the race and ethnicity of children with disabilities served under IDEA Part B*. U.S. Department of Education. https://sites.ed.gov/osers/2021/08/osep-releases-fast-facts-on-the-race-and-ethnicity-of-children-with-disabilities-served-under-idea-part-b/

16 National Center for learning disabilities. (n.d.). *Significant Disproportionality in Special Education: Current Trends and Actions for Impact*. https://www.ncld.org/wp-content/uploads/2020/10/2020-NCLD-Disproportionality_Trends-and-Actions-for-Impact_FINAL-1.pdf

17 Wagner, Roger D. (1991). A historical analysis of Federal Statutes, Rules, and Court Cases related to the expulsion of handicapped children: Recommendations and criteria for policy development. *Dissertations*. 3162. https://ecommons.luc.edu/luc_diss/3162

18 Brylan Advocates LLC. (n.d.). *The "Stay Put" Provision Explained*. Brylan Advocates. https://brylanadvocates.com/the-stay-put-provision-explained/

19 Florida Department of Education. (n.d.). *Florida Statute/Rules for Discipline*. Florida Department of Education. https://www.fdle.state.fl.us/MSDHS/Meetings/June-Meeting-Documents/Presentations/

June-7-1045AM-DOE-Olivia-School-Discipline.aspx#:~:text=www.
FLDOE.org,-8&text=(4)(c)%20Zero%E2%80%90,vandalism%20of%20
less%20than%20%241%2C000

20 Jefferson County Public Schools. (2013–2014). Code of acceptable behavior and discipline and the student bill of rights. II_
DRAFT201314CodeOfConductUpdated062013_0.pdf

21 Omaha Public Schools. (2022–2023). Code of Conduct. (2022–2023).
Retrieved from https://www.ops.org/Page/548

22 Nevada Department of Education: Standardized Definitions for
Student Discipline Offenses and Sanctions. (June 2022). Retrieved
from https://doe.nv.gov/uploadedFiles/ndedoenvgov/content/
Boards_Commissions_Councils/StatewideSchoolSafetyTaskForce/
2022/December/AB490(2019)StandardizedDefinitions06.18.2022.
pdf

23 National Center on Safe Supportive Learning Environments. (June
30, 2022). Nevada compilation of school discipline laws and regu-
lations. *United States Department of Education*. Retrieved from
https://safesupportivelearning.ed.gov/sites/default/files/discipline-
compendium/Nevada%20School%20Discipline%20Laws%20
and%20Regulations.pdf

24 Missouri Department of Elementary and Secondary Education.
(2023). What is "Special" about Special Education? Specially designed
instruction for students with varying exceptionalities within a Multi-
tiered system of supports. Retrieved from https://dese.mo.gov/
media/pdf/what-special-about-special-education

25 Brown, T. (November, 2022). Florence one schools' zero-tolerance policy for fighting under investigation: NAACP. Retrieved from: https://
wpde.com/news/local/florence-one-schools-zero-tolerance-policy-
fighting-under-investigation-naacp

26 Houston Independent School District Code of Conduct. (2012–2013).
Retrieved from https://www.houstonisd.org/Page/78683

27 U.S. Department of Education, EDFacts Data Warehouse (EDW): "IDEA
Part B Child Count and Educational Environments Collection," 2018–
19. https://www2.ed.gov/programs/osepidea/618-data/state-level-
data-files/part-b-data/child-count-and-educational-environments/
bchildcountandedenvironments2018-19.csv

28 Thompson, J. (2016). Eliminating zero-tolerance policies in schools:
Miami-Dade County public schools' approach. *Brigham Young
University Education and Law Journal*, *2016*(2), 325–350.

29 U.S. Department of Education, IDEA. (2022, July 10). New guidance helps schools support students with disabilities and avoid disparities in the use of discipline. https://sites.ed.gov/idea/new-guidance-helps-schools-support-students-with-disabilities-and-avoid-discriminatory-use-of-discipline/

30 U.S. Department of Education, Office of Special Education and Rehabilitative Services (OSERS). (2022, July 19). Positive, proactive approaches to supporting children with disabilities: A guide for stakeholders. https://sites.ed.gov/idea/files/guide-positive-proactive-approaches-to-supporting-children-with-disabilities.pdf

31 Testa, M., & West, S.G. (2010). Civil commitment in the United States. *Psychiatry (Edgmont)*, *7*(10), 30–40. PMID: 22778709; PMCID: PMC3392176

32 Shea, T., Dotson, S., Tyree, G., Ogbu-Nwobodo, L., Beck, S., & Shtasel, D. (2022, August 12). Racial and ethnic inequities in inpatient psychiatric civil commitment. *American Psychiatric Association*. https://doi.org/10.1176/appi.ps.202100342

33 St. George, D. (2023, March 16). In Florida, showing mental health struggles could ger a child detained. *The Washington Post*. https://www.washingtonpost.com/education/2023/03/16/florida-law-child-mental-health/

34 St. George, D. (2023, March 16). In Florida, showing mental health struggles could ger a child detained. *The Washington Post*. https://www.washingtonpost.com/education/2023/03/16/florida-law-child-mental-health/

35 Paksarian, D., Mojtabai, R., Kotov, R., Cullen, B., Nugent, K.L., & Bromet, E.J. (2014, February 1) Perceived trauma during hospitalization and treatment participation among individuals with psychotic disorders. *Psychiatric Services, 65*(2), 266–9. https://doi.org/10.1176/appi.ps.201200556

36 St. George, D. (2023, March 16). In Florida, showing mental health struggles could ger a child detained. *The Washington Post*. https://www.washingtonpost.com/education/2023/03/16/florida-law-child-mental-health/

37 Evans, J., & Reeves, M. (2019, December 10). Florida's flawed Baker Act rips thousands of kids from school. https://www.tampabay.com/news/education/2019/12/10/floridas-flawed-baker-act-rips-thousands-of-kids-from-school/

2

Assessments and RELD Students in Special Education

Kayla is an eight-year-old, third-grade Biracial American student who was diagnosed with attention deficit/hyperactivity disorder (ADHD) and a specified learning disability (SLD). In the middle of the year, Kayla has not scored higher than a 62% on her Reading Benchmark Assessments. Kayla's teacher, Ms. Thomas, thinks Kayla has more potential, but is not trying. When Ms. Thomas pulls Kayla to small group reading, she constantly has to repeat directions and redirect Kayla. Lately, Kayla has been more distracted and oftentimes doesn't complete her classwork. Concerned about Kayla making academic progress and meeting criteria for promotion, Ms. Thomas speaks with the ESE support facilitator, Ms. Henry, for suggestions. During the meeting with Ms. Henry, Ms. Thomas learns that Kayla is currently homeless. Also, Ms. Henry explains to Ms. Thomas that she suspects that Kayla has dyslexia, but the mom has not been able to get her officially tested because the school does not provide that kind of testing. Ms. Henry shares some resources on dyslexia and agrees that Kayla has potential, but it takes patience. Ms. Thomas walks out of the meeting with a new perspective and restructures her lesson plans so she can maximize Kayla's potential.

Testing and assessing can be an issue for many students and is known to be a concern for students with varying exceptionalities.[1] However, for years, education policies have been enacted

DOI: 10.4324/9781032648965-2

to emphasize high expectations for all, which requires standard-ized testing and educational professionals' accountability for students' proficiency. The Education Title I of Elementary and Secondary Education Act of 1965 (ESEA) required states and school districts to assess students and evaluate local programs in order to receive Title I funding. The law offered "grants to dis-tricts serving low-income students, federal grants for textbooks and library books, funding for special education centers, and scholarships for low-income students."[2] This act was supposed to improve academic achievement for disadvantaged students. However, based on assessments, schools continued to struggle to improve academic achievement for students.

In 1983, a report called *A Nation at Risk* claimed that American schools were failing due to mediocrity and requested that educators, parents, and students help reform public schools. According to the education data, four major topics were a focus: content, expectations, time, and teaching. The report compared American schools and colleges to other advanced nations and studied the connection between college admissions require-ments and student high school achievement. The report found that around 23 million American adults are functionally illiter-ate; among minority youth, functional illiteracy could be as high as 40%, and the average achievement of students on standard-ized tests was much lower compared to decades ago. Concerned with other countries matching and surpassing America's educa-tional attainments, experts made suggestions. Among the many suggestions were improvements in high school curricula, new textbooks, and an emphasis on standardized assessments.[3] The *Nation at Risk* report resulted in corporate and state leaders rais-ing academic standards and creating standardized testing.[4]

A Nation at Risk paved the way for the No Child Left Behind (NCLB) Act of 2002, under the George W. Bush administration, which also stressed the importance of high expectations and clos-ing the achievement gap among traditionally underserved stu-dents by stressing high accountability. The law required states to report students' assessment scores by race and income level. In 2015, the 1965 Title I Act was amended under the Every Student

Succeeds Act (ESSA), where schools were required to submit a plan that revealed challenging academic standards, implementation of exceptional academic assessments, and a statewide accountability system. The Obama administration supposedly granted more flexibility to states and districts with the newly enacted ESSA.[5] Also, in 2009, Obama created the Race to the Top program, which funded millions of dollars to school districts who focused on improving teaching and learning. In order for districts to receive funds from this competitive grant, they had to implement plans to help improve assessments, hold schools to more rigorous standards, turn around deteriorating schools through increased resources, provide educational support to help educators be more effective, and improve methods to help track progress of students and teachers.[6] Education of disadvantaged students was not only the focus of the government, but it appeared to be the top priority of many wealthy individuals. Billion-dollar foundations also supported standardized testing and accountability measures.

For example, the Eli & Edythe Broad Foundation education work focused on urban areas with students from low socioeconomic status, and they backed Denver's 1999 pay-for-performance requirement, which focused on achievement gains on standardized assessments.[7] Likewise, the Gates Foundation focused on quantifiable results, despite a Gates Foundation informant's view of the foundation's focus on solving problems without understanding the context.[8] Foundations drive numerous education policies, and if districts want funds to support their schools, they must abide by specified rules. There are numerous foundations that have a say in multiple education policies without truly understanding the needs of disadvantaged youths. In theory, these policies, supporters, and grants are supposed to help improve outcomes for students from underserved schools, but the reality is that they only exacerbated issues within many school districts.

The Race to the Top funded 12 states (Delaware, District of Columbia, Florida, Georgia, Hawaii, Maryland, Massachusetts, New York, North Carolina, Ohio, Rhode Island, and Tennessee), which were awarded millions of dollars—Florida and New York received the largest amount, $700 million. Many New York principals protested the new teacher evaluation system. Additionally, New York increased the rigor of its assessments and aligned them closely to Common Core standards. Common Core standards are skills students should have at each grade level in language arts and math.[9] The state made its English and math assessments more challenging, which caused proficiency rates to plummet. In Florida, standardized assessments were implemented for every subject including art, music, and physical education.[10] A few years after being awarded the Race to the Top grant, Florida implemented end-of-course (EOC) exams for high schools, which are 30% of high school students' grades. If they fail the exam, they could potentially fail the class and as a result, have to retake the exam in order to move forward with subsequent classes. In the District of Columbia (D.C.), the teachers union did not support the new teacher evaluation system; the union claimed that it promoted winners and loser rather than cooperation. Also, the assessment system was changed to align with Common Core standards. In the Race to the Top grant application, D.C. promised to close the minority achievement gap by 5% points each year.[11] Evidence shows that the grant caused friction in some states and caused all states to create rigorous assessment requirements, which only added to the stress of students and educators alike.

At underserved schools there are a plethora of concerns that are not placed at the forefront of education. Many students at disadvantaged schools belong to demographic groups that are at a higher risk of experiencing traumas. Research reveals that youth living with intellectual and developmental disabilities (IDD) experience exposure to trauma at a higher rate than their non-disabled peers. Additionally, many homeless youths are also victims of violence or other traumatic events.[12] Black students are said to be twice as likely to be identified as having emotional disturbances and intellectual disabilities than their non-Black peers while American Indian students are said to be twice as likely to be identified as having specific learning disabilities and four times as likely to be identified as having developmental delays. Also, Black students are 40% more likely and American Indian students are 70% more likely to be identified as having disabilities than their peers.[13] To add to the overidentification of minority groups being diagnosed with a high incidence disability, most minority groups suffer from homelessness. African Americans make up 13% of the general population, but more than 40% of the homeless populations.[14] A majority, if not all, underserved schools are filled with minorities from the aforementioned groups, that is, racially, ethnically, and linguistically diverse students and students with varying exceptionalities. Education policies do not look at the whole picture, and most politicians have neither taught inside today's classrooms nor experienced the lives of students with varying exceptionalities. Due to federally mandated state assessments aligned with content standards, many school districts push assessments throughout the school year to ensure all students are on track to grade level proficiency.

In the largest school district, New York City, K–12 students are required to take assessments several times throughout the school year. Periodic assessments are used to keep track of students' academic success. Also, for elementary schools, New York local and state assessments are administered to support instruction and provide information on students' progress toward mastering grade level standards.[15] Florida has some of the largest school districts in the nation, specifically, the sixth largest school district, Broward County. Similarly to New York City, schools are required to administer periodic assessments for reading, math, and science. Elementary school students are given benchmark assessments several times throughout the year and progress monitoring assessments three times a year.[16] Houston Independent School District (HISD) administers periodic assessments and local and state assessments as well.[17] Assessing students is not inherently negative; assessments serve a purpose: tests inform instruction and allow educators to see areas where students may need assistance or intervention. However, with over-testing and accountability measures, less time is being dedicated to actually teaching students and more time is being focused on teaching to a test. James Baldwin once said, "a teacher who is not free to teach what he wants is not a teacher." Educators have not had autonomy in their own classrooms for a long time, and cannot prepare students to think for themselves.

In order to meet the needs of students with varying exceptionalities more adequately, educators would have to take a more holistic route —focus on children's intellectual, emotional, physical, and spiritual needs—to teaching. As professor of education Peter Taubman once expressed, "We lose sight of the painfully beautiful, impossibly complex student before us" in focusing on excessive formal and standardized assessments.[18] Additionally, Diane Ravitch once said in the *National Standards in American Education*, if standards are the goal, then there are three types of standards that should work together prior to testing. These standards include the content standards, which describe what teachers are supposed to teach and what students are expected to learn; the performance standards, which define the levels of mastery of content students need to attain; and the opportunity to learn, that is, the programs and resources schools and districts provide to support teachers in helping students to meet the standards.[19] According to this model, school districts are lacking in the third suggested standard, which is the opportunity to learn. Many resources are out there for educators, but educators can't make sufficient use of them because they are consumed with formal assessments.

As a former educator working with RELD students with varying exceptionalities, I witnessed how assessments placed many students under great distress. At times my students have had mental breakdowns, crying outbursts, and enraged emotions because they are overwhelmed by testing. As mentioned above, many students at disadvantaged schools face multiple traumas; over-assessing children with varying exceptionalities does not help professionals face the critical issue at hand— trauma. Trauma can disrupt encoding and processing memory. Traumatized children experience additional insult by performing poorly in school and as a result, the school is now not a place the child deems safe.[20] A traumatized person in a state of alarm is less capable of focusing, more anxious, and more attentive to nonverbal cues such as tone of voice, body stance, and facial expressions.[21] It is evident that persistent assessments contribute to the depreciation of our children's self-esteem. Ultimately, the agenda of these policies adds to the inequalities within our educational system. Policy makers and district leaders ask for an accumulation of data from tests to examine students' growth and proficiency levels, as well as to compare districts and/or states. However, this process of data collection does not conduce to students' or educators' mental well-being. Educators should be able to focus on students' overall well-being in order to make progress toward closing the achievement gap between disadvantaged populations of students and their privileged counterparts. Since changing deeply rooted education policies is not a plausible option, what can educators do to improve academic outcomes for RELD students with varying exceptionalities?

To reach children with trauma and varying exceptionalities, educators must be able to gain their attention. Various attention tasks can help improve students' academic outcomes. When a child is chronically inattentive, there is an issue with their executive functioning skills. Executive functioning skills are mental skills that involve "attention, problem solving, flexible thinking, working memory, self-control, and emotional control."[22] Executive function skills are needed for learning, behavior, and overall development. Selective and sustained attention tasks can help improve students' reading and reading comprehension. Sustained attention is imperative for reading comprehension because a student must retain information and make necessary connections within a text.[23] For a sustained attention task, an educator can have a student read a passage and set a timer for a specified number of minutes. S/he can allow a student to complete an activity of his/her choice for 10–15 minutes followed by an unappealing task such as reading and answering comprehension questions. It is important for educators to make directions clear and concise with more than one presentation format[24] and to improve selective attention, which is the ability for an individual to focus on one task while noise or other distractions occur. A child can read a story with a target word, and every time the word is read, the student can complete an action such as writing a number or something similar. As the child's attention improves, the educator can make the activity more challenging by asking comprehension questions from the story.

There are multiple attention tasks for students with memory deficits and learning disabilities.[25] Moreover, to better assist students with attention and memory difficulties, educators can wait longer after giving instructions to allow longer processing time and provide information visually as well as orally. Similarly, educators can partake in errorless learning, which is when educators ask questions but provide the answers before inaccurate deducing occurs. Educators can have students engage in spaced retrieval tasks by having a child read a story and the teacher immediately asking a comprehension question. Later, the teacher asks the same question, and over time, the question is progressively spaced out.[26]

Furthermore, for students with SLD such as dyslexia, educators can change the display of instruction, such as text size, font, reduced color contrast—colors that diminish visual glare, such as tranquil greens and blues.[27] The size of the stems on letters like b an p plays a major role for students with dyslexia. Students with dyslexia rely on remembering shapes of words, and when letters are difficult to distinguish from one another, it may result in inaccurate word recognition and reading difficulties. To better assist students with dyslexia, educators can provide students with color overlays. Color overlays are more common for digital material but can be used for printed material. In California, for online testing, students have the option to change the color contrast; it would help if all states were required to provide color overlay accommodation for students with SLD. Last, it is helpful to have images on documents; it helps alleviate students' stress when students are required to read a lengthy body of text.[28] The abovementioned attention tasks and visual accommodations can assist students with varying exceptionalities to achieve academic outcomes. Before attention activities take place and accommodations are made, it is beneficial to make sure the child is in the state of mind to want to learn.

Before engaging in learning, students should participate in mindfulness activities. Much is required of educators, so it is easy to forget to check in with students. I believe mindfulness activities should be completed once in the morning and once in the afternoon to maintain children's engagement and at the end of the day before they exit the classroom. Mindfulness activities can also take place when students seem to appear severely distracted. Some school districts adopted social emotional learning (SEL) activities, but all schools and/or teachers do not follow activities with fidelity. For example, at a middle school where I volunteered, the principal took a minute of silence for the mindfulness activity, but mindfulness activities are much more than that. From practicing breathing techniques to counting down, students can learn to recognize and manage their thoughts, emotions, and actions. Belly breathing is an excellent technique for students battling anxiety or aggression issues, and it promotes relaxation. Likewise, students can take brain breaks by engaging in a calming activity such as coloring or drawing. There are numerous mindfulness activities to optimize students with varying exceptionalities' learning experiences.

Ms. Thomas started her work week with a new perspective and fresh ideas to better assist Kalya. Ms. Thomas shifted her lesson plans so she could have one-on-one time with Kayla twice a week. During Kalya's one-on-one instruction, Ms. Thomas administered short passages to Kayla and asked her simple W-questions—what, when, who, why, and where. Before the start of each reading activity, Ms. Thomas allotted ten minutes for Kayla to complete a free choice activity. Once the ten minutes were up, Ms. Thomas reviewed the rules with Kayla verbally and provided the rules in print, which were pasted on the table. After three weeks of 25 minutes on Mondays and Fridays with Kayla, Ms. Thomas noticed positive changes in Kayla's mood. Kayla started to approach reading with an optimistic outlook. However, Ms. Thomas was still concerned about Kayla's aptitude to pass the end of the year standardized reading assessment.

Standardized assessments are biased and designed for students with privileged upbringings. Many passages assigned on standardized assessments contain common knowledge for middle-class White students, whereas marginalized groups lack the background knowledge to truly comprehend the text. Prior knowledge makes a high difference in students' ability to understand a passage. Unfortunately, minority students from low socioeconomic backgrounds' positive worldly experiences are few and far between. At one point, I worked one-on-one with a student on a reading assignment. The only way he could make sense of the word "restrained" was by explaining to me what he witnessed in his neighborhood relating to police officers and civilians. Oftentimes, the experiences of underserved individuals are not positive, and the positive experiences they do have are not the dominant group's experiences; therefore, assessments created by a dominant group do not suit marginalized groups.

To expose children to variety and a wider range of knowledge, educators could focus on integrating topics through passages. Exposure to more science and social studies topics can provide students with a wealth of knowledge that can help improve their academic performance on standardized tests. Read-alouds are commonly conducted in primary grades, but I think it is an activity that should occur throughout secondary school. To interest RELD students with varying exceptionalities in different topics, educators should read books on specific topics and allow time for open discussions. Also, using academic words on a daily basis can help students adopt a larger vocabulary. For example, to teach the word "habitat," an educator can utilize that word in their everyday language while working with students and also display the word on their word wall. Repetition is key to academic improvement, so if the abovementioned activities are completed daily, progress is sure to be made.

Racially, ethnically, and linguistically diverse students in special education who lack exposure to a wider range of knowledge is not the only issue hindering their progression. Since 2021, a growing number of states have implemented certain classroom censorship bills that restrict conversations about race and gender in K–12 classrooms. Many school districts are banning books— mostly books about Black, Indigenous, and people of color, and the lesbian, gay, bisexual, transgender, intersex, queer, and asexual (LGBTIQA) community—from school libraries and requiring educators to scan their books through a system to make sure they are acceptable. Students not being exposed to relatable books or books that dive into their racial and cultural history can decrease their sense of belonging. A sense of belonging is a feeling of safety, support, acceptance, inclusion, and identity. A sense of belonging impacts academic and social performance, and when RELD students with varying exceptionalities do not feel they belong, their academic performance can be adversely impacted.

The implementation of more than 100 bills across the nation placed critical race theory (CRT) under heavy scrutiny. Critical race theory is a framework that focuses on how systemic racism is deeply rooted in and shapes American society. As a result, many opposing politicians of CRT view any discussions concerning race and sexuality to be disconcerting. Florida, Texas, South Carolina, Indiana, Tennessee, Idaho, New Hampshire, and Oklahoma are just a few states among many that have implemented censorship bills. These various bills have drastic penalties that can adversely impact educators' jobs; educators can face termination for holding certain discussions.[29] In Florida, a school district temporarily barred the film *Ruby Bridges* after a parent's complaint. A couple of parents complained that the film could teach students that "White people hate Black people."[30] *Ruby Bridges* is a book I read to my students every year; instead of viewing the story as an account of a young Black overcoming adversity, parents of a dominant group decided to view it as a story that teaches hate. Stories, films, and conversations on various accounts of Black history and on Hispanic and Asian culture, and the like, are crucial in helping students gain a stronger sense of self.

RELD students with varying exceptionalities—specifically, emotional and behavioral disorders—experience a great deal of self-loathing that triggers low self-esteem and self-hate.[31] Teaching RELD children with severe disorders about individuals from marginalized groups overcoming difficulties can teach these students to love themselves and face hardship with a positive mindset. Sharing my story—alone—with my students shifted their mindset and resulted in my students working harder to meet their academic achievement goals. I witnessed my students going from zero ounces of hope to sharing their dreams of becoming lawyers, computer engineers, and the like. Unfortunately, many great stories of successful minorities or individuals from marginalized groups are about them overcoming racism, sexism, fascism, classism, and so forth, but those stories can encourage and empower individuals who lose sight of hope. So how can educators work around these punitive bills?

The U.S. Department of Education (USDOE) leaves curriculum concerns up to state and local education officials. Therefore, these bills are not necessarily a concern nationwide—as of yet—but many states are affected. What educators should understand about these bills is that this does not mean to reframe from being culturally responsive, but it does mean that educators must move strategically to avoid termination or suspension. In Florida, the Stop Wrong to Our Kids and Employees (WOKE) Act, also known as the Individual Freedom Act (IFA), prohibits teaching and instruction that teaches that: (*a*) members of one race, color, national origin, or sex are morally superior to members of another race, color, national origin or sex, (*b*) a person by advantage of his or her race, color, national origin, or sex is inherently racist, sexist, or oppressive—consciously or unconsciously, (*c*) a person's status as either privileged or oppressed is determined by his or her race, color, national origin, or sex, (*d*) members of one race, color, national origin, or sex cannot attempt to treat others without respect to race, color, national origin, or sex, (*e*) a person by advantage of race, color, national origin, or sex should receive adverse treatment because of actions committed in the past by other members of the same race, color, national origin, or sex, (*f*) a person by advantage of race, color, national origin, or sex must feel guilt or psychological distress because of actions committed by a person of the same race, color, national origin, or sex, (*g*) benefits like merit, excellence, hard work, fairness, objectivity, racial colorblindness are racist or sexist, or were created by members of a particular race, color, national origin, or sex to oppress members of another race, color, national origin, or sex.[32]

As mentioned above, Florida's bill—similar to other laws in other states—is very detailed and warns educators not to touch on sensitive topics surrounding race and sexuality, but it does not mean that educators must avoid racial and cultural topics as a whole. Educators can read literature that shines light on positive experiences of RELD individuals such as sharing Imhotep's—an Egyptian architect—contributions in Africa, can teach students about various Hispanic scientists such as Carlos Juan Finlay, and the like. Educators can share optimistic stories without touching on racial, sexual, and cultural conflict, and including certain literature can turn on a light bulb in many RELD students with varying exceptionalities, which can lead these students to seek knowledge on their race and culture outside of school. So once again, to reiterate, students can still be reached through culturally responsive teaching; literature just must uphold a positive light on people of various ethnic origins.

Kayla has found a new love for science since Ms. Thomas discovered multiple books online concerning famous Black scientists. Kayla's favorite book was *Mae among the Stars*, a book about Mae Jemison (Black female astronaut who studied chemical engineering). Ms. Thomas intermixed nonfiction and fiction science stories to expose Kayla to various academic terms such as observation, habitat, astronomy, gravity, and so forth. In whole group, she shared various fiction stories that teach children positive social and emotional responses as well as ethical building (well-known standards of right and wrong). She read *Did I Ever Tell You How Lucky You Are?* as well as *Horton Hears a Who!* by Dr. Seuss, and she could tell that Kayla was really interested in the books because during their whole group discussions, Kayla actively participated. As Kayla's optimism improved, so did Ms. Thomas's, and as school progressed, so did Kayla's performance. She still had some struggles, but she just received her first passing score on her Benchmark Reading assessment. Although the school year was almost toward the end, Ms. Thomas felt that Kayla would continue to make academic improvements.

Imagine working at a school where general educators in primary grades usually have a class that comprises 18–21 students, where 30% of students may have individualized education plans and 47% of students may be going through response to intervention (RTI). For intermediate grades, general educators usually have a class that comprises 21–25 students where 33% of students may have IEPs and 44% of students may be going through the RTI process. In both scenarios, only 23% of students are without accommodations. All educators have plenty on their plate, but educators in high-needs schools are overwhelmed with helping students meet grade level standards. Additionally, in high-needs schools, educators have the added pressure to close a wide achievement gap, so assessments are piled on students that cause instruction to be less free flowing and more focused on specified standards. I must note that assessments are not inherently negative, but over-assessing students, especially students with burdened trauma, is a concern. Taubman once said that "the more we busy ourselves with designing set curricula, with perfecting exams, and testing out new hypotheses, with locating 'best practices' for some generic student, the more we risk keeping things exactly as they are."[33]

Educators must work within the parameters they are given, but there are ways to maximize RELD students with varying exceptionalities' academic achievement within the limits. Using mindfulness and exposing RELD students with varying exceptionalities to a wider range of knowledge can help combat the issues that occur due to implementation of rigid bills, competitive grants, and federal education polices. I understand the importance of evolving with time, and implementing necessary tools for our students' success, but assessing our students frequently is not evolution; it is deterioration. We must focus on the mental well-being of our children to truly see them prosper throughout their educational career.

Notes

1 The National Center for Fair and Open Testing. (2017, March 30). Does inclusion in testing mean inclusion in meaningful learning? https://fairtest.org/standardized-testing-and-students-disabilities/#:~:text=When%20students%20with%20disabilities%20are,as%20a%20certificate%20of%20completion

2 U.S. Department of Education. (n.d.). *Every Student Succeeds Act (ESSA)*. https://www.ed.gov/essa?src=rn

3 Gardner, D. (1983). A nation at risk: The imperative for educational reform. An open letter to the American people. A Report to the nation and the secretary of education. *Department of Education*. https://files.eric.ed.gov/fulltext/ED226006.pdf

4 Russakoff, D. (2015). *The prize: Who's in charge of America's schools?* Houghton Mifflin Harcourt.

5 U.S. Department of Education. (n.d.). *Every Student Succeeds Act (ESSA).* https://www.ed.gov/essa?src=rn

6 Chen, G. (2022, May 19). What is race to the top and how will it benefit public schools? *Public School Review.* https://www.publicschool review.com/blog/what-is-race-to-the-top-and-how-will-it-benefit-public-schools

7 Tompkins-Stange, M.E. (2016). *Policy patrons: Philanthropy, education reform, and the politics of influence.* Harvard Education Press.

8 Tompkins-Stange, M.E. (2016). *Policy patrons: Philanthropy, education reform, and the politics of influence.* Harvard Education Press.

9 Gewertz, C. (2015, September 30). The Common Core explained. *Education Week.* Retrieved from https://www.edweek.org/teaching-learning/the-common-core-explained/2015/09

10 Boser, U. (2012, March). Race to the top: What have we learned from the states so far? A state-by-state evaluation of race to the top performance. *Center for American Progress.* https://files.eric.ed.gov/fulltext/ED535605.pdf

11 Boser, U. (2012, March). Race to the top: What have we learned from the states so far? A state-by-state evaluation of race to the top performance. *Center for American Progress.* https://files.eric.ed.gov/fulltext/ED535605.pdf

12 The National Child Traumatic Stress Network. *Populations at risk.* https://www.nctsn.org/what-is-child-trauma/populations-at-risk

13 Child Trends. (2017, January 12). *5 things to know about racial and ethnic disparities in special education.* https://www.childtrends.org/publications/5-things-to-know-about-racial-and-ethnic-disparities-in-special-education

14 National Alliance to end Homelessness. (2020, June 1). *Racial inequalities in homelessness, by numbers.* https://endhomelessness.org/resource/racial-inequalities-homelessness-numbers/

15 NYC Public Schools. (n.d.). *Periodic Assessments.* https://www.schools.nyc.gov/learning/testing/periodic-assessments

16 Broward County Public Schools. (n.d.). *Statewide and District Assessments.* https://www.browardschools.com/testingcalendar

17 Sam Houston Math, Science, and Technology Center High School. (n.d.). *Testing: Texas*. Sam Houston Math, Science, and Technology Center. https://www.houstonisd.org/domain/47717

18 Taubman, P. (2000). Teaching without Hope. *Journal of Curriculum Theorizing*. http://www.ncbi.nlm.nih.gov/pubmed/8822346

19 Ravitch, D. (1996). *National Standards in American Education: A Citizen's Guide* (p. 255). Brookings Institution Press.

20 Perry, B.D. (2006). Fear and learning: Trauma-related factors in the adult education process. *New Directions for Adult and Continuing Education, 2006*, 21–27. https://doi.org/10.1002/ace.215

21 Perry, B.D. (2006). Fear and learning: Trauma-related factors in the adult education process. *New Directions for Adult and Continuing Education, 2006*, 21–27. https://doi.org/10.1002/ace.215

22 The OT Toolbox. *Executive Functioning*. https://www.theottoolbox.com/executive-functioning-skills/

23 Macdonald, K.T., Barnes, M.A., Miciak, J., Roberts, G., Halverson, K.K., Vaughn, S., & Cirino, P.T. (2020, October 8). Sustained attention and behavioral ratings of attention in struggling readers. *National Library of Medicine: National Center for Biotechnology Information, 25*(5), 436–451. https://doi.org/10.1080/10888438.2020.1826950

24 South County Child & Family Consultants. *Improve sustained attention*. https://southcountychildandfamily.com/resources/executive-functions/sustained-attention/

25 The OT Toolbox. *Attention activities*. https://www.theottoolbox.com/attention/

26 Johnson, R. (2018). Trauma and learning: Impacts and strategies for adult classroom success. *MinneTESOL Journal, 34*(2), 1–9. http://minnetesoljournal.org/wp-content/uploads/2018/11/Johnson-2018-Trauma-and-Learning_-Impacts-and-Strategies-for-Adult-Classroom-Success.pdf

27 Full Fabric: Education. *How to design visual learning resources for neurodiverse students*. https://www.fullfabric.com/articles/how-to-design-visual-learning-resources-for-neurodiverse-students

28 Full Fabric: Education. *How to design visual learning resources for neurodiverse students*. https://www.fullfabric.com/articles/how-to-design-visual-learning-resources-for-neurodiverse-students

29 American Civil Liberties Union. (2022, March 10). Defending our right to learn. Retrieved from https://www.aclu.org/news/free-speech/defending-our-right-to-learn

30 Bellamy, C. (2023, March 28). Florida elementary school temporarily bars 'Ruby Bridges' film following parent's complaint: A parent at North Shore Elementary complained that the film might teach students about white people hating black people. *NBC News*. Retrieved from https://www.nbcnews.com/news/nbcblk/florida-elementary-school-temporarily-bars-ruby-bridges-film-parents-c-rcna76924

31 Ogundele, M.O. (2018, February 8). Behavioral and emotional disorders in childhood: A Brief overview for pediatricians. *National Library of Medicine: National Center for Biotechnology Information, 7*(1), 9–26. https://doi.org/10.5409/wjcp.v7.i1.9

32 Vile, J.R. (2022, November 22). Stop W.O.K.E. Act (Florida). *The First Amendment Encyclopedia*. https://www.mtsu.edu/first-amendment/article/2167/stop-w-o-k-e-act

33 Taubman, P. (2000). Teaching without Hope. *Journal of Curriculum Theorizing*. http://www.ncbi.nlm.nih.gov/pubmed/8822346

3

Disproportionality and Culturally Sustaining Practices

Rodney is a nine-year-old, third grade Black American student who was retained in kindergarten in hope that he would catch up to his peers and who later was diagnosed with attention deficit hyperactivity disorder (ADHD). However, he is still not meeting grade level standards, and his third grade teacher, Mrs. Moore, continues to complain to the Exceptional Student Education support facilitator about Rodney's behaviors. At times in the classroom, Rodney randomly screams during whole group instruction, leaves his assigned seat frequently, and often is placed in isolation from his peers due to his inappropriate social behaviors. Rodney has a hard time making friends because during recess, he hits his classmates to get their attention. Academically, Rodney is below grade level; he recognizes letters and sounds, he can read three-to-four letter words, but he struggles with multisyllabic words and comprehension. In math, he is on grade level; during whole group instruction, he actively participates. According to Mrs. Moore, the math lesson is the only time she can get Rodney's undivided attention. When Mrs. Moore conferenced with Rodney's mother concerning his behavioral issues and academic deficits, his mother claimed that Rodney was not receiving the help he needed. Rodney's mother was a single mother living in a low-socioeconomic neighborhood

DOI: 10.4324/9781032648965-3

and experienced homelessness prior to enrolling Rodney in school. Mrs. Moore felt that Rodney should be re-evaluated for a self-contained emotional behavioral disorder (EBD) classroom.

Luis is a nine-year-old, fourth grade Hispanic student who moved from Tulum, Mexico, to San Diego, California, when he was seven years old. According to the resource teacher at Palm Elementary, Luis is an L3 English language learner, which means he can use and understand a series of English-related sentences in oral conversations. At home, Luis is the oldest sibling out of three and the only child attending grade school. Luis's parents understand and speak only Spanish. Sometimes, Luis finds himself responding to his English-speaking teacher, Mrs. Watts, in Spanish because he struggles with transitioning from home to school. Furthermore, Luis is struggling in reading/language arts and having a difficult time reading fluently and comprehending. Mrs. Watts complained to the ESOL resource teacher, Mrs. Garcia, that she has a difficult time reaching Luis and explained that Luis is failing her class and has failed multiple language arts assessments. Mrs. Watts is curious to know if Luis should be placed in response to intervention and possibly placed in a varying exceptionalities classroom.

In 1954, *Brown vs. Board of Education* was deemed to have changed the lives of many African Americans in the South by dismantling racial segregation as well as paving the way for students with varying exceptionalities to receive an equal educational opportunity. There has been constant evolution within the American education school system. However, schools are still racially segregated, and 70% of students attend their neighborhood school, schools that lack essential resources.[1] Additionally, White American and Native American students with varying exceptionalities tend to be included in general education settings more often than African American, Asian, and Pacific Island students with varying exceptionalities.[2] Segregation of students with intellectual and developmental disabilities is a major issue in America.[3] To add insult to injury, although the number has somewhat decreased, African Americans remain the highest proportion of students placed in special education under intellectual disability (ID) and Emotional Disturbance (ED) status.[4]

Likewise, Hispanic students in California were labeled with ID at an alarming rate.[5]

Moreover, in 1968, the Bilingual Education Act (BEA) was implemented to address the needs of bilingual students. It was eventually incorporated into the Every Student Succeeds Act (ESSA), which concentrates on closing the achievement gap between English Language Learners (ELLs) and other students.[6] However, in recent years, even with the implementation of ESSA, some school districts still struggle to meet the needs of ELLs.[7] In California, the numbers of Hispanic students referred to special education under the label of intellectual disability were largely due to inappropriate testing.[8] English Language Learners are the fastest-growing group of students in grades K–12 in the United States and by 2025, one out of four children in classrooms across the U.S. will be classified as an ELL.[9] ELLs are held to the same standards as English-speaking students, regardless of their proficiency levels, but studies revealed that ELLs are still achieving significantly lower scores on their language arts assessments compared to their English-speaking peers.[10] Research suggests that the increase of Hispanic students diagnosed with a learning disability (LD) may have something to do with the increase of ELLs in U.S. public schools.[11] Students of color and students from low-socioeconomic backgrounds tend to be disproportionality placed in special education programs due to cultural mismatch, poverty, problematic programming, and curriculum.[12] Similarly, ELLs are being placed in a dire situation where they are expected to meet grade level standards with limited English proficiency, ultimately causing them to be mislabeled and misdiagnosed. In this case, disproportionality occurs when students' representation in special education programs or specific special education category surpasses their proportional enrollment in schools' general population[13] or when there are too few of a specific group of people referred to specialized placement. As previously mentioned, RELD students are overrepresented in multiple subjective categories under the Individuals with Disabilities Education Act (IDEA). Regardless of disability category, African American students tend to have fewer positive outcomes than their White counterparts.[14] Many American education practices and curricula are inappropriate for RELD students and tend to mute their voices due to master scripting: the dominant culture's classroom practices, pedagogy, instructional materials, and theoretical paradigms; master scripts are grounded in Eurocentric and White supremacist ideologies.[15] Master scripting distorts worldly occurrences unfavorable to White supremacy and subjects students to stereotypical ideations. Also, RELD students are subjected to a curriculum that lacks rigor, which results in more students of color being referred to special education.[16] This chapter seeks to present interdisciplinary culturally sustaining frameworks through fictitious scenarios that can help better support RELD students and decrease disproportional representation in special education.

There are many RELD students like Rodney and Luis, students who may have been misdiagnosed, misunderstood, or mislabeled due to cultural differences. Likewise, numerous educators like Mrs. Moore and Mrs. Watts are not always given the necessary tools and resources to better assist students like Rodney and Luis. So, how can one remedy the issues that plague RELD students? Sometimes, in American schools, RELD students lose their cultural identity due to assimilation and being educated by predominantly White middle-class females (79%),[17] where they are required to adhere to an "American" standard. In the United States, many deficit-teaching approaches view languages, literacies, behaviors, and cultural roots of students of color as inadequacies, and the only way to overcome these "inadequacies" is by them learning the dominant language (English), literacy (English print), "proper" decorum (White American standards), and cultural ways (American).[18] RELD students are placed in a position where they are expected to assimilate when they really should be accommodated. Under the umbrella of culturally relevant pedagogy (CRP) exists CSP, which is a framework that focuses on sustaining linguistic, literate, and cultural pluralism. In other words, students would be able to successfully progress with their cultural upbringing intact while existing in a dominant culture (American).[19] Culturally sustaining frameworks require educators to dismantle social structures placed in schools, abandon preconceived notions about RELD students, and focus on building upon students' strengths to help overcome educational inequities. It is critical to note that CSP and/or CRP frameworks are not synonymous with critical race theory (CRT). Critical race theory is an intellectual movement that focuses on the idea that race is not natural and biological, but instead a socially and culturally constructed notion that is used to oppress and exploit Black and Brown individuals. Critical race theory advocates believe that racism is innate in the law and legal systems within the United States, which creates social, economic, and political inequalities between minorities and their White peers.[20] As mentioned above, CSP and CRP are essentially focused on children maintaining their cultural backgrounds while attending schools that uphold a different culture.

Rodney displayed behaviors aligned with ADHD, but it could have been a case of misdiagnosis. Research found that African American children were 5.1 times more likely to be misdiagnosed with a conduct disorder before being diagnosed with autism spectrum disorder (ASD).[21] RELD students are oftentimes excluded from their general education peers due to improper diagnoses. Diagnoses of externalizing behaviors lead to future dropout rates as well as suspension and incarceration rates. To improve Rodney's academic outcomes, it would behoove Mrs. Moore to seek more culturally relevant pedagogy. Hip-hop pedagogy sparks interest in our urban youth. Although hip-hop is heavily scrutinized, it gives voices to urban cultures, which arose from a socio-political movement in the 1970s—it is an outlet for many Black and Latinx children.[22] Hip-hop based education (HHBE) uses elements and feelings of hip-hop culture to enlighten formal and informal educational spaces.[23] Hip-hop can be used to promote youths' literacy skills through critiquing hip-hop songs and poems as well as helping provide RELD students with a stronger sense of self.

The five categories of hip-hop include masters of ceremonies (MCing), graffiti art, breakdancing, disk jockeying, and knowledge of self, but it also includes pedagogical approaches.[24] In an academic classroom, the MCs will be the students and teachers, who both serve as masters of content (the academic content). In hip-hop, MCing can be done in two different ways: there can be co-MCs or there can be a "call-and-response" situation, where one artist (teacher) can perform a musical statement or rhythm (the call) and another person (students) can respond to the statement with another rhythm or statement (the response). When there are two MCs or co-teachers (teacher and student), the student who agreed to be the co-MC will have to take home the lesson plan to review in order to teach the class the next day. The teacher reviews the content with the student prior to the lesson to ensure that the student understands how the content will be delivered, and the student is responsible for adding their delivery style to the lesson plan. Hence, the student becomes the master of the content. During class, the teacher sits in the student role and raises a hand to ask questions as the content is being delivered. Co-MCing gives students more autonomy and helps them gain an in-depth understanding of the content to be learned. "Call-and-response" delivery requires the teacher to actively call on students. For example, if the teacher says, "If you can hear my voice, scream" (the call), the students scream in unison (the response).[25] In the song *Happy* by Pharrell Williams, there is a call, and then musical instruments are played (the response), a prime example of how "call-and-response" works. In teaching HHBE, MCing is what draws the students in to the topic at hand. In African culture, "call-and-response" is one of the main foundations for vocal and lyrical communication.[26]

Historically, graffiti art has been a code of communication for minorities; they write codes to convey information such as where to find food or shelter without being discovered by higher-ups. In the United States, hip-hop travels back to the 1970s, when youths from inner cities like New York, Chicago, Los Angeles, and Washington, D.C., wrote on walls, freight trains, and the like to satisfy their need for a sense of belonging. Participating in graffiti art was an alternative to being a part of a gang.[27] Graffiti art is a form of abstract expression that can be unreadable to the human eye and have multiple meanings. Across cities, artists will "tag" or put their name in various areas to spread their name around. Also, graffiti art is a way to express individuality and to challenge mainstream notions of what represents art.[28] The graffiti art element of hip-hop can provoke thoughts and emotions.[29]

Educators can use visual arts so students can make personal connections about their judgments and feelings. In science, the element of graffiti art can help a student identify a specified concept. A teacher can present a picture of lightning or a storm to identify different transformations of energy. Visual arts can help students make connections to evidence-based texts in reading, science, and history. Students can also create graffiti art to help explain what they have read, which will help them gain a deeper understanding of a given passage. Research study completed on HHBE found that students preferred graffiti art over reading and copying notes from textbooks.[30]

To satisfy kinesthetic learners, breakdancing in hip-hop allows learners to move their bodies when connecting to the literature—in the form of songs or poems and/or connecting to science lessons. Breakdancing is also referred to as "b-boy," "b-girl," and "breaker" and has four kinds of movement: top-rock, down-rock, power moves, and freezes.[31] Up-rock is a form of breakdancing where two dancers mimic ways of fighting in rhythm with the music. Down-rock is when breakdancers focus on footwork and ground movements. Power moves are break-dancers spinning on their hands, heads, shoulders, and/or elbows. Last, freeze occurs when the breakdancer pauses in a movement; the breakdancer holds the position, oftentimes at the end of a performance.[32] Educators can have students move around to display different states of matter. For solid, students can gather closely together and freeze; for liquid, students can move slowly apart, and for gas, students can move fast and remain far apart.[33] Also, for breakdancing, educators can have students display certain movements to explain certain scenes in a given text. Acting out information from a text as the teacher reads aloud can help students better understand the passage.

In hip-hop, the DJ feeds off the MC and helps bring the students' interests and voices into the classroom. The disc jockey oversees the energy in the room by creating the playlist. Students can oversee the music/poetry that is played or read in class, and they can continue to add to the list through the school year. A playlist can be used in various subjects like social studies and science. According to one research article, an educator had students create a playlist for a unit on race relations in the United States. The educator created a list of critical questions that guided the playlist. On the playlist, songs were connected to specified race issues in America; "King Kunta" connected to Black perseverance and ingenuity, "For Free" was linked to reparations, and "The Blacker the Berry" was associated with anti-Blackness. For the song, "King Kunta," the educator asked students the following questions: How does Kendrick Lamar describe the attitude of Black men in America? Who do you think King Kunta is? Students discussed their responses in a small group. Subsequently, students engaged in small learning stations to examine Kunta Kinte in the movie *Roots* and identify dominant sources of information about people who were enslaved and exemplified the characteristics of persistence and resourcefulness.[34] In this study, the educator was able to tap into students' critical thinking skills by using a playlist that spoke on race topics. DJing is a crucial role in hip-hop, but it is not the last essential role in hip-hop.

The core of hip-hop is knowledge of self; hip-hop is a culture that stresses the importance for individuals to be aware of self, to be authentic, and to be confident in who they are. Knowledge of self concentrates on students' lived experiences, and through HHBE students can liberate themselves by engaging in critical thinking skills within classroom spaces they co-created. In a government class, the educator asked her students to identify critical issues based on their personal experiences that adversely impacted their communities. Some students identified environmental issues such as lead in their city's water, which resulted in students finding ways to help their community (i.e., contacting their state representatives). Students developed new skills such as understanding, writing, and ratifying legislation and how to reach out to individuals in their community.[35] Knowledge of self allowed students to advocate for themselves and their communal environments.

The five elements of hip-hop do not have to be interdependently used. An educator can decide to use one part of the five elements to teach a lesson. They can utilize MCing, graffiti, breakdancing, DJing, or knowledge of self to teach reading, science, math, art, and so forth. The use of HHBE can improve school climate by making RELD students feel accepted and appreciated.

However, it is vital for educators to analyze their position (i.e., how do they feel about hip-hop and its influence on culture?) when before implementing HHBE. Also, educators should ask students about their perspective on hip-hop prior to implementing hip-hop related classroom lessons.

After conferencing with Rodney's mom, Mrs. Moore felt defeated and decided to vent to one of her colleagues. She felt the mom was not receptive to her concerns, and she did not have any clue as to how to reach the student. Her colleague, a highly effective educator, suggested that Mrs. Moore focus on finding various ways to connect with Rodney. Mrs. Moore did not know where to start, however. After researching for a couple of weeks, Mrs. Moore found a way to decrease Rodney's behaviors and spark his interest in reading. To improve his reading comprehension skills, Mrs. Moore used music lyrics. One morning, while Rodney was walking to the classroom, he heard upbeat music coming from Mrs. Moore's class, specifically, the sound of a piano and guitar; as he approached the door, words followed, and he heard a familiar rapper's voice. As Nas's lyrics flowed, other children enthusiastically walked in the classroom. Mrs. Moore paused the song once everyone was seated and introduced the assignment, "Today class, we are going to analyze a song call 'I can' by a hip- hop artist called Nas. I am going to play the song once without the lyrics, then, I am going to play it with the lyrics, and the third time, we are going to carefully break the lyrics apart without the musical sound in the background. Sound good, class?" While the song played, she allowed students to get out of their seats so they could feel the music. Although it was unconventional, Mrs. Moore was excited because she noticed that Rodney was particularly enthusiastic. Mrs. Moore asked how they felt after listening to the music without the lyrics. when the students listened to the music with the lyrics, Mrs. Moore scanned the room to see if kids attempted to sing the words, and finally, when she played the lyrics, Mrs. Moore asked students what they thought the overall theme was for the song. Rodney exclaimed that the song meant be the best you can be., Mrs. Moore joined Rodney in a smile. She became more confident in her abilities to keep Rodney engaged, and Rodney started to put more trust in his teacher.

As shown in Luis's scenario, sometimes it is difficult for ELLs to maintain one language while in school. Mrs. Watts suspected a disability due to Luis's language barrier. As mentioned above, ELLs are also frequently misdiagnosed. If Mrs. Watts incorporated more culturally sustaining pedagogy in her everyday lessons, then she might see better performance from Luis. Translanguaging is a culturally sustaining pedagogy that allows students to use their native language as a resource without concerns for boundaries between the different languages. Instead, they are able to modify the use of language resources based on various communicative contexts to bring all information to full coherency. Translanguaging pedagogy influences students' home language to improve their academic performance.[36] Additionally, translanguaging allows parents to engage more in their child's homework when schools use the child's home language. As a result, educators can rejoice in the fact that their ELLs are progressing at a faster rate.[37] Translanguaging can be compared to a spinning top with different colors on it where the colors are representative of different languages the student may speak. When students are permitted to freely speak their home language as a resource, it is like a spinning top: they are able to show their true identify and knowledge.[38] In practice, educators can create a collaborative space for bilingualism where students can express their multilinguistic identities and develop a wide range of meaning-making through interactions with peers while the educator serves as a social agent or facilitator.[39]

For example, a student could be reading literature about the solar system in English, but take notes or respond to questions in Spanish. Also, some other activities that can possibly support translanguaging are delivering vocabulary lessons in various languages, which are called collective translation chances. Another way translanguaging can be used is to use home-language word equivalencies. If two students are working together on math word problems in English and one student becomes puzzled, the students can identify a similar word in their home language so the math word problem is coherent.[40] It is important to understand that translanguaging and translation are not one and the same. Translanguaging goes beyond general translations. An individual can engage in translanguaging by participating in translation activities, but the translation activity is not word-for-word. Students use their home language to make sense of English words, then respond in English once they comprehend. Unlike translations, translanguaging help learners understand the composition of English writing.[41] During translanguaging, learners gain a better understanding of subject-verb agreement, the placement of adjectives, and the like. It is important to note that educators do not have to speak the same language as the student to engage in translanguaging. Also, translanguaging does not hinder ELL students' ability to acquire the English language; it actually helps students gain an in-depth understanding of the English language by making vital connections between their home language and English.

After Mrs. Watts spoke with the ESOL resource teacher, Mrs. Garcia, she decided to build a stronger relationship between her proficient bilingual students so she could provide a collaborative space for all of her students with hopes of improving Luis's academic progress. Because Luis struggled with reading comprehension and the class was currently working on figurative language, Mrs. Watts asked one of her higher achieving bilingual students to share some popular Spanish idioms. During planning time, Mrs. Watts typed a variety of popular Spanish and English idioms, cut them up, and placed them in a jar for her students to pull from the next day. When the time came, students were placed in heterogeneous groups with at least one academically proficient bilingual student. Luis pulled from the jar first and found a Spanish idiom and read it to his group:, "Tener memoria de pez," which translates as "To have a memory of a fish." Mrs. Watts observed the groups working together and witnessed Luis's immediate laughter as if he understood the idiom, Joanna—taken aback by Luis's laughter—asked "what does that mean?" and Luis responded in Spanish, "tener mala memoria." Joanna repeated Luis's response in English, and said, "Oh, it means to have a bad memory," and the group joined Luis in laughter. Excited to learn, Luis continued to participate as he acquired a deeper understanding of idioms. Mrs. Watts smiled as she observed Luis's progress and later decided to incorporate

Spanish and English in reading instruction and focus on historical contexts such as early civilizations like the Mayan Empire, which was formed in Tulum, Mexico. Mrs. Watts concluded that if Luis could connect to what he is learning, he would be able to be more productive and produce work that revealed his true capabilities.

Two distinct examples of CSP were provided, but the aforementioned examples are not the only ways to engage in CSPs. Educators can engage in CSP by exploring nontraditional texts (i.e., student writing, poetry, videos, blog posts, memes, etc.). Nontraditional texts challenge the idea of what counts as reading and writing in public schools.[42] Furthermore, educators can encourage students to explore other cultural associations outside of their dominant subcultural group (i.e., culture of the city they are from, exceptionality and/or non-exceptionality, place of work, etc.).

The overrepresentation and identification of marginalized students in special education continues to be a consistent issue in American school systems. Various issues such as test bias, cultural mismatch between student and teacher, and curriculum infrastructure all contribute to the disproportionate number of students of color being referred to specialized programs. Culturally sustaining pedagogies can better assist educators in meeting the needs of RELD students with and without varying exceptionalities. Hip-hop based education and translanguaging are two distinct culturally sustaining pedagogies mentioned in this chapter, but the overarching purpose of CSP is to welcome multiple perspectives, connect students to their real-life experiences, provide students from various walks of life with a stronger sense of self, and encourage student-centered learning. Likewise, CSP can help decrease the number of RELD students being referred to special education and, as a result, balance the scales.

Notes

1 Carillo, S., & Salhotra, P. (2022, July 14). *The U.S. student population is more diverse, but schools are still highly segregated.* NPR. https://www.npr.org/2022/07/14/1111060299/school-segregation-report

2 National Council on Disability. (2018, February 7). *IDEA Series: The Segregation of Students with Disabilities*. https://ncd.gov/sites/default/files/NCD_Segregation-SWD_508.pdf

3 Lewis, L. (2021, November 5). Opinion: Developmentally disabled students are in schools, but so is segregation. *Colorado Community Media*. https://coloradocommunitymedia.com/stories/developmentally-disabled-students-are-in-schools-but-so-is-segregation,384619

4 Zhang, D., Katsiyannis, A., Ju, S., & Roberts, E. (2014). Minority representation in special education: 5-year trends. *Journal of Children Family Studies, 23*, 118–127. https://doi.org/10.1007/s10826-012-9698-6

5 Blanchett, W., Klinger, J., & Harry, B. (2009). The intersection of race culture, language, and disability: Implication for urban education. *Urban Education, 44*(4), 389–409. https://doi.org/10.1177/0042085909338686

6 National Education Association. (2020, July). *English Language Learners*. National Education Association English Language Learners | NEA.

7 Schleeter, G., Slate, J., Moore, G., & Lunenburg, F. (2020). Reading inequities by the economic status of Texas grade 3 English language learners: A Texas, multiyear analysis. *Journal of Education and Learning (EduLearn), 14*(1), 34–46. https://doi.org/10.11591/edulearn.v14il.13893

8 Blanchett, W., Klinger, J., & Harry, B. (2009). The intersection of race culture, language, and disability: Implication for urban education. *Urban Education, 44*(4), 389–409. https://doi.org/10.1177/0042085909338686

9 National Education Association. (2020, July). *English Language Learners*. National Education Association English Language Learners | NEA.

10 Miley, S.K., & Farmer, A. (2017). English language proficiency and content assessment performance: A comparison of English learners and Native English speakers' achievement. *English Language Teaching, 10*(9), 198–207. https://doi.org/10.5539/elt.v10n9p198

11 Sullivan, A.L. (2011). Disproportionality in special education identification and placement of English language learners. *Exceptional Children, 77*(3), 317–334.

12 Artiles, A. (2019). Re-envisioning equity research: Disability identification disparities as a case in point. *Educational Researcher, 48*(6), 325–335. https://doi.org/10.3102/001389X19871949

Blanchett, W., Klinger, J., & Harry, B. (2009). The intersection of race culture, language, and disability: Implication for urban education. *Urban Education, 44*(4), 389–409. https://doi.org/10.1177/0042085909338686

Utley, C., Obiakor, F., & Bakken, J. (2011). Culturally responsive practices for culturally and linguistically diverse students with learning disabilities. *Learning Disabilities: A Contemporary Journal, 9*(1), 5–18. https://www.proquest.com/scholarly-journals/culturally-responsive-practices-linguistically/docview/881457980/se-2?accountid=10901

13 Blanchett, W.J. (2006). Disproportionate representation of African American students in special education: Acknowledging the role of White privilege and racism. *Educational Research, 35*(6), 24–28.

14 Blanchett, W.J. (2006). Disproportionate representation of African American students in special education: Acknowledging the role of White privilege and racism. *Educational Research, 35*(6), 24–28.

15 Swartz, E. (1992). Emancipatory narratives: Rewriting the master script in the school curriculum. *Journal of Negro Education, 61*(3). https://doi.org/10/2307/2295252

16 Blanchett, W.J. (2006). Disproportionate representation of African American students in special education: Acknowledging the role of White privilege and racism. *Educational Research, 35*(6), 24–28.

17 National Center of Education Statistics. (2020, September). *Race and Ethnicity of Public School Teachers and their Students*. https://nces.ed.gov/pubs2020/2020103/index.asp

18 Paris, D., & Alim, H.S. (2014). What are we seeking to sustain through culturally sustaining pedagogy? A loving critique forward. *Howard Educational Review, 84*(1), 85–100. https://doi.org/10.17763/haer.84.1.982l873k2ht16m77

19 Paris, D., & Alim, H.S. (2014). What are we seeking to sustain through culturally sustaining pedagogy? A loving critique forward. *Howard Educational Review, 84*(1), 85–100. https://doi.org/10.17763/haer.84.1.982l873k2ht16m77

20 Britannica, T. Editors of Encyclopedia. (2023, August 11). Critical race theory. Encyclopedia Britannica. https://www.britannica.com/topic/critical-race-theory

21 Rentz, C. (2018, March 19). Black and Latino children are often overlooked when it comes to autism. *NPR*. https://www.npr.org/sections/health-shots/2018/03/19/587249339/black-and-latino-children-are-often-overlooked-when-it-comes-to-autism

22 Margolis, L. (2000, February 11). Hip-Hop gives voices to urban culture. *The Christian Science Monitor*. Retrieved from https://www.csmonitor.com/2000/0211/p15s1.html

23 Adjapong, E. (2021). Exploring hip-hop pedagogy for the advancement of girls of color in science. *Urban Education, 56*(6), 843–871. https://doi.org/10.1177/00420859211000090

24 Chang, J. (2007). *Can't stop won't stop: A history of the hip-hop generation*. St. Martin's Press.

25 Adjapong, E.S., & Emdin, C. (2015). Rethinking pedagogy in urban spaces: Implementing hip-hop pedagogy in the urban science classroom. *Journal of Urban Learning Teaching and Research, 11*, 66–77. https://files.eric.ed.gov/fulltext/EJ1071416.pdf

26 Benjamin Groff. *Using call-and-response in your songs (history, examples & today's hits)*. https://www.benjamingroff.com/blog/call-and-response#evolution

27 Rahn, J. Painting without permission: An Ethnographic study of hip-hop graffiti culture. https://journals.lib.unb.ca/index.php/mcr/article/view/17784/22155

28 CSDT. *Graffiti orgins*. https://csdt.org/culture/graffiti/origins.html

29 Wei, M.T., Yang, Z., Wang, X., Liu, D.X., Bai, Y.J., Guo, R.Y., Yu, N., & Ling, X. (2023). Pitfalls of hip hop pedagogy: Re-examining and questioning the definition. *Frontiers in Psychology, 14*, 1135808. https://doi.org/10.3389/fpsyg.2023.1135808

30 Adjapong, E.S. (2017). Bridging theory and practice: Using hip-hop pedagogy as a culturally relevant approach in the urban science classroom.

31 History of hip hop. *Breakdancing/b-boying/breaking*. https://historyofthehiphop.wordpress.com/hip-hop-cultures/break-dancingdance/

32 The Breaks: A Breaking Encyclopedia. *Freeze*. https://thebreaks.org/articles/freeze.html

33 Adjapong, E. 5 ways to use hip hop in the classroom to build better understanding of science. *The Conversation*. https://theconversation.com/5-ways-to-use-hip-hop-in-the-classroom-to-build-better-understanding-of-science-160737

34 Allen, K. (2023). Activating hip-hop pedagogy in the social studies classroom. *National Council for Social Studies, 87*(3), 172–177. https://www.socialstudies.org/system/files/2023-06/se-8703172.pdf

35 Allen, K. (2023). Activating hip-hop pedagogy in the social studies classroom. *National Council for Social Studies, 87*(3), 172–177. https://www.socialstudies.org/system/files/2023-06/se-8703172.pdf

36 Son, Sangsok. (2021). *The Multilingual Classroom*. Translanguaging in Education. About | Translanguaging Education.

37 Son, Sangsok. (2021). *The Multilingual Classroom*. Translanguaging in Education. About | Translanguaging Education.

38 Son, Sangsok. (2021). *Two States of TL Top*. Translanguaging in Education. About | Translanguaging Education.

39 Gort, M., & Sembiante, S.F. (2014). Navigating hybridized language learning spaces through translanguaging pedagogy: Dual language preschool teachers' languaging practices in support of emergent bilingual children's performance of academic discourse. *International Multilingual Research Journal, 9*(1), 7–25. https://doi.org/10.1080/19313152.2014.981775

40 Najarro, I. (2023, July 13). What is translanguaging and how is it used in the classroom? *Education Week*. https://www.edweek.org/teaching-learning/what-is-translanguaging-and-how-is-it-used-in-the-classroom/2023/07

41 Najarro, I. (2023, July 13). What is translanguaging and how is it used in the classroom? *Education Week*. https://www.edweek.org/teaching-learning/what-is-translanguaging-and-how-is-it-used-in-the-classroom/2023/07

42 Machado, E. (2017, May 31). Culturally sustaining pedagogy in the literacy classroom. *International Literacy Association*. https://www.literacyworldwide.org/blog/literacy-now/2017/05/31/culturally-sustaining-pedagogy-in-the-literacy-classroom

4

Prevalent Issues Impacting RELD Families and Educators

A single mother of three, Natasha Williams from Trinidad has been frustrated for over six months now because her son's school is "dragging their feet" about re-evaluating her son, Damian, who was diagnosed with ADHD, oppositional defiance disorder (ODD), and a mood disorder. According to his mother, he is a bright young boy. Ms. Williams provided the school with the diagnosis, and they explained to her that their psychologist works twice a week, but the school never followed up with a meeting date. Since her son, Damian, started the second grade, Ms. Williams has been receiving complaints from his teacher, Mrs. Garcia. Mrs. Garcia complained that Damian ripped pages from books, tapped on his keyboard, did not follow directions, interrupted the class with noises, and was defiant. For months, Ms. Williams has been receiving bad reports, and her son has been receiving disciplinary actions such as suspensions, but the school still has not made any progress toward a re-evaluation meeting. Currently, Damian is failing in all subjects, and Mrs. Garcia does not know how to work with Damian's behaviors. Ms. Williams asked the school for accommodations or a change of setting, but without an IEP, the school could not provide necessary accommodations. It is now February, and Ms. Williams has grown intimidated by the school due to their lack of responsiveness—the

DOI: 10.4324/9781032648965-4

school has yet to schedule a meeting with Ms. Williams, and her son's behaviors and grades have not improved. As a result, Ms. Williams reached out to a friend of hers—a special education teacher—who directed her to a parent advocacy center to better assist her with her needs.

According to the IDEA §1450.11 (findings), Congress finds parent training and activities to assist parents of a student with varying exceptionalities with dealing with the stress of parenting with a particular concentration in (a) occupying a vital role in generating and upholding positive connections between parents of children with varying exceptionalities and schools by facilitating open communication between the parents and schools, assuring dispute resolution at the earliest possible time, and discouraging the intensification process between parents and schools, (b) guaranteeing the involvement of parents in scheduling and decision-making in regard to early intervention and educational and transitional services, (c) attaining high-quality early intervention, educational, and transitional results for children with varying exceptionalities, (d) delivering parents their procedural safeguards and responsibilities to guarantee improved early intervention, educational, and transitional results for children with varying exceptionalities, (e) supporting parents in developing skills to effectively partake in the education and development of their child and the transition process, (f) supporting the roles of parents as participants within partnerships looking to improve early intervention, educational, transitional services, and results for children with varying exceptionalities, and (g) assisting parents who may have limited access to services and support due to economic, cultural, and/or linguistic barriers.[1]

Parents' training and activities are needed for parents of RELD students with varying exceptionalities, but oftentimes, they are not made aware of their role as a parent to speak up on behalf of their child. Parent advocacy is when the parent asks questions, raises concerns, asks for help, and teaches their child to speak up for themselves. Oftentimes, for true advocacy to take place, parents must trust someone at the school so they can feel confident enough to speak on issues and concerns.[2] Moreover, it is imperative for parents to keep an organized record of all their child's data, that is, assessments, messages from teachers, any information from meetings, homework, and schoolwork that their child may have completed. Also, parents should understand their child's overall strengths, weaknesses, likes and dislikes, so they can share information with the child's teacher. Parents should understand federal, state, and local laws concerning children with varying exceptionalities early on so they can effectively communicate on their child's behalf.[3] Lack of parent advocacy is a growing concern in schools where parents are from RELD backgrounds and low-socioeconomic status. Unfortunately, students with varying exceptionalities from more affluent families have greater chances of having a positive educational experience due to parent advocacy. Due to strong parent advocacy from White affluent families, school districts tend to be more responsive to parents' concerns so they do not run the risk of being sued.

In New York City, wealthy White families from affluent backgrounds sued the New York City school board for not properly implementing the IDEA.[4] After the lawsuit, they were able to provide a privatized and higher quality education for their children with varying exceptionalities.

Social-cultural capital—social (relationships and social networks) and cultural (material items and knowledge)—is a plausible reason for the lack of parent advocacy among RELD parents of students with varying exceptionalities. Social-cultural capital permits individuals to access valuable resources. Parents who do not have power and/or social and cultural status struggle to gain access to the same resources and high-quality education as more affluent families. With social-cultural capital, RELD parents can gain the emotional and social support they need to assist in reaching their advocacy goals.[5] Depending on racial, ethnic, cultural, and/or linguistic makeup, parent advocacy needs and concerns may look vastly different. There are four different kinds of parent advocates: intuitive advocates, disability experts, strategists, and systemic change advocates. RELD parents from low-socioeconomic backgrounds tend to utilize intuitive advocacy—advocates who take the "I know my child" approach—which is not a powerful approach toward advocacy. Unfortunately, oftentimes, educators disregard parents' point of view when they are solely expressing their suggestions and concerns from an intuitive perspective.[6] The strategist approach is less likely to be utilized by RELD families but appears to be an approach that is most helpful for parents. The strategist frequently utilizes sophisticated knowledge surrounding IDEA, their understanding of their child's exceptionality, parental rights, documents, and procedural safeguards. Also, strategists understand the role they can play in making decisions about referrals, evaluations, accommodations, and inclusion. Last, change agents are usually privileged because they have access to informational resources and personal connections to educators and administrators.[7] As an educator, your responsibility is to verbally educate your parents on parent advocacy and the best methods and ways to advocate.

From experience as an elementary special educator for RELD students with emotional and behavioral disorders, I found that explaining to parents the importance of advocating for their child was not always easy—especially when there was a conflict of roles. Conflict occurs when two or more roles are incompatible. As educators, we are supposed to side with the professional, but then we have our own personal beliefs that sometimes interfere with decisions of other professionals. One of my students was recommended for a behavioral center when he transitioned to middle school, but I did not agree with the decision nor did the parent. However, as a professional, I had to be on the same page as my ESE specialist so it would not be a major issue if the parent wanted to go to due process. During the entire ordeal, data were consistently being collected on the student, and unfavorable comments were made, and when the student's guardian contacted me, I had to remain neutral. However, the ESE specialist questioned whether or not I had spoken with my student's guardian to make her outwardly express her issues with the decision to place her child in a special behavioral center. The parent asked me about the school, and I openly and directly explained my feelings, but I did not advise her on what to do. While my feelings about my student were apparent to all administrative staff, I did not have to steer the guardian in a certain direction because she had relatives in the education field whom she asked for advice. In the position of an educator, I find it is important to drive your parents to advocate, but one must be aware of any conflicts and effectively communicate to parents without becoming defensive toward one side or the other. It is best to state the facts when speaking with parents and direct them to resources and/or groups that do not have any conflict of interests or roles.

In order to increase parent advocacy in high-needs schools, educators and other personnel must build a bridge between home and school. Good communication is the most effective route to creating a trusting relationship with RELD families of students with varying exceptionalities. Collaboration is when people work together to achieve a common goal, and when educators work with parents, together they improve children's behavioral, social, and academic outcomes. Studies have revealed that parents' participation leads to optimistic outcomes for children with varying exceptionalities. Racially, ethnically, and linguistically diverse parents from low-income communities tend to collaborate with educators when the educator initiates communication.[8] However, for RELD families, it has been challenging for parents and teachers to build successful relationships. Parents with children with varying exceptionalities often feel as if the educators do not want to collaborate when their child is having complications in the classroom.[9] In a study completed in Tennessee and Illinois, Hispanic parents protested that educators did not consistently communicate, and during IEP meetings, parents felt bullied and dismissed when they offered suggestions concerning their child. Many Spanish- and English-speaking parents complained that general education teachers were not well versed and lacked professional skills needed to work with RELD students with varying exceptionalities.[10] One of the barriers that adversely impacts parent-teacher relationships is that educators do not always listen to or value parents' contribution.[11] As previously mentioned, educators have the responsibility of making parents feel comfortable to speak up about any of their concerns, and the only way an open line of communication can occur between parents and educators is if there is a level of trust. When I worked with RELD students with varying exceptionalities, I was able to build trust quickly by sharing my personal background. Parents appreciated my transparency and competency while students appreciated my honesty. I listened to parents' concerns without judgment, but also made clear my position and responsibilities as a teacher. Experiences with parents were not always sunshine and rainbows, but in the end, most parents appreciated my communication and collaboration efforts.

For instance, I had a multicultural student in the fourth grade who had severe ADHD. He loved math and was competitive, so he always wanted to do his best. However, he struggled in reading due to his inability to remain focused for long periods of time. Also, he had difficulties with spelling words from third grade high-frequency vocabulary. His dad's biggest concern was spelling, and he made sure he called me constantly about his child's lack of spelling skills. I listened to his concerns and implemented spelling tests, but spelling was not my top priority. My number one priority was teaching my student reading comprehension techniques and writing because I knew he had great potential and could pass the standardized assessment at the end of the year. The child's dad tended to go on belligerent rants, and one time, verbally disrespected my assistant principal. I faced multiple verbal attacks from the child's dad, but I was never perturbed by his behavior; he simply was impulsive and emotional. However, once he verbally attacked my assistant principal, I chose to call him to have a conversation concerning my responsibility as his son's teacher and his responsibility as a father. I explained to him that spelling skills for high-frequency words occur at the primary level, and as an intermediate educator, I was more concerned about his comprehension skills. Additionally, I explained to the dad that he was his child's first teacher and foundation. I explained that I was doing the best I could, but he would have to be an active participant as well. At the end of the school year, that same student received a level 4 on his Writing Assessment and went from a level 1 (in third grade) to a level 4 in reading and math. The dad profusely thanked me and said, "You are the first teacher to care about my child" and apologized for his behavior throughout the year.

The abovementioned story was an example of an ongoing battle with a parent, but I remained transparent, honest, and respectful during the many uphill battles I endured with him.

As an educator, you must not take any outbursts personally and always remain professional and true to your purpose. I can openly admit that I had moments of frustration, but each day, I went in to work with a new mindset and new ways to assist all my students and parents. Parents may not always be well versed and have impeccable knowledge of the IDEA, but it is up to the educator to explain to parents the best ways to advocate for their child. I may not have reached every family, but I connected with the majority of parents, and most of the times, I connected successfully; other times, I was not as successful as I wanted to be. Reaching at least 70% of RELD students and families with varying exceptionalities is a cause for celebration. RELD parents from low-socioeconomic backgrounds have multiple stressors, as do educators, but as an educator it is your job to step outside of yourself when working with overwhelmed parents who do not have insight into the educational process.

Stepping outside of yourself requires humility and an open mind. From experience, I found myself having to step outside of myself frequently. In one occurrence, a mom grew increasingly upset with me because I sent her a late second IEP meeting reminder on the day of the meeting. Honestly, I did not think to send another reminder earlier on because I sent home paperwork weeks before. The mom texted me that she had six kids, work, and much on her to-do-list so she would not be able to attend the meeting and asked to reschedule. Additionally, she expressed her annoyance with me for sending the message at the last minute. I responded, apologizing and explaining my point of view, but did not contain her frustration. I worked with the parent for multiple years, and multiple times she was annoyed by my actions or responses, but because we cultivated a level of trust in the beginning, our partnership in improving her child's behavioral and academic outcomes remained resilient. In the aforementioned scenario, Mrs. Garcia had not tried to build a relationship with Ms. Williams. Mrs. Garcia's complaints caused Ms. Williams to seek outside assistance so she could better advocate for her child.

Ms. Lisa, who works at a local parent advocacy center, reached out to Ms. Williams and expressed her sincerest empathy. Ms. Lisa had been the confused and hopeless parent when her own child was diagnosed with autism and she had no one to assist her through the IEP and educational process. Ms. Williams, relieved to finally talk to someone who understood her frustration, poured out all her feelings concerning her child. Ms. Lisa listened carefully without interrupting Ms. Williams and jotted down major points. After Ms. Williams finished venting, Ms. Lisa proceeded to ask questions about Ms. Williams's knowledge of her child's diagnoses and her expectations and provided her with known resources and explained the assessment process. Ms. Lisa assisted Ms. Williams with drafting an email to the ESE specialist and also explained that she should make a follow-up phone call. Ms. Lisa ensured Ms. Williams that she would be by her side during the re-evaluation meeting when it was officially scheduled.

During the virtual meeting, which occurred a couple of weeks after Ms. Williams reached out to the advocacy center, Ms. Lisa professionally expressed her dismay with the school's lack of urgency to assist Damian so he could have a quality education. It was toward the end of the year, and Damian—a bright boy—had failed all his subjects. The ESE specialist, Ms. Benson, apologized and proceeded with the meeting. At the conclusion of the meeting, Ms. Williams became more aware of the process, and Ms. Lisa explained the next steps to Ms. Williams. The school year has been exasperating for Ms. Williams, but Ms. Lisa eased Ms. Williams's mind by reminding her that there would be better days ahead for Damian.

Ms. Williams's experience with Damian's current school and educator resembles the experiences of many RELD families of students with varying exceptionalities. Educators are viewed as experts in the field due to their degrees and familiarity with curriculum. Once teachers begin teaching curriculum that is unfamiliar to parents, teachers are seen as having special expertise in pedagogy, so parents' experiences are no longer valued. As time progresses, home and school connections became more disconnected when parents focused more on teaching their child their ethnicity and family origins and less on their child's school curriculum. In urban areas, parents from low-socioeconomic backgrounds were viewed as incapable, and educators would often play the role of the mother and teach children various skills and help build children's self-esteem.[12] However, the widened gap between home and school has not benefited anyone—parents, educators, and students alike. The cultural disconnect between families and educators results in RELD students in special education receiving a low-quality education. Educators tend to develop preconceived notions about children from dissimilar cultural and socioeconomic backgrounds; as a result, RELD students are seen as behaviorally unfit and/or academically below standards. Known scholars and educators in the field of education, Dr. Beth Harry and Dr. Maya Kalyanpur revealed techniques to remedy the issues schools and families face when working with RELD families in special education. A term coined in the 1990s, *cultural reciprocity* expressed a way to build successful relationships with RELD families of children with special needs.

According to Drs. Kalyanpur and Harry, in order for educators and service providers to display reciprocity, they must engage in personal reflection; invite, listen to, and respect the parents' views; engage in full reciprocity with parents by explaining professionals' assumptions and beliefs; and collaborate reciprocally. Personal reflection is when you—the educator—ask yourself questions such as (*a*) What is the basis of assessment and recommendation for someone's child? (*b*) Do you value the parents' knowledge, or do you only value scientifically based knowledge that comes from professional training? When respecting parents' views, you listen to the parent and invite any suggestion, you must view adverse conversations as disagreements, not as if the parent is in denial. Educators should explain their point of view as a professional then, last, collaborate without academic jargon and try to meet in the middle for the betterment of the child.[13] Cultural reciprocity prevents stereotyping and guarantees that both parents and educators are empowered and strive for subtle levels of awareness of differences. There is overt, covert, and subtle awareness: overt is obvious differences such as language or the way someone dresses; covert is an awareness that cannot be recognized by outward signs and subtly involves identifying embedded values and beliefs that underlie people's actions and an awareness that one's beliefs have been taken for granted and assumed universal. In order to be culturally reciprocal, educators have to think of their own culture; culture makes up national-ity, race/ethnicity, gender, social class, religion, exceptionality/non-exceptionality, and the like. One's culture does not remain stagnant, but changes with one's experiences. Culture is what provides most individuals with their worldview.[14] Therefore, the culture of individuals who have obtained degrees and who are from middle-high-class families may look vastly different from individuals who have dropped out of high school or never attended college and are from low-socioeconomic backgrounds. So, as an educator, you must acknowledge your worldviews; share your views, but refrain from forcing your views on the parents of your students.

In America, there is a dominant culture (national macro-culture)—a culture where people who belong to this culture do not have to define, explain, or differentiate themselves to any-one since they belong to a culture whose ways and rules are the guidelines of the society. Under the macroculture, there are microcultures, cultures that are shared by a small group of peo-ple with limited perspectives. There are even various cultures within education; we have general education culture and special education culture, and oftentimes, the perspectives of individ-uals who are a part of the special education culture are vastly different from the perspectives of individuals who are a part of the general education culture. However, a conflict in views does not mean resolutions cannot be reached. Racially, ethnically, and linguistically diverse parents, especially RELD parents whose first language is different from the dominant culture's language, tend to remain quiet when conversing about their child's social, academic, and/or emotional status, and this lack of communica-tion sometimes result in unfavorable outcomes for their child.[15] Educators must help give parents power to help make decisions about their child.

During the IEP process, parents are asked about their child's progress and how they think their child is doing overall. But are parents' thoughts really being considered during the educa-tional process or are professionals just typing information into a box for compliance? In education, we are constantly thinking about satisfying legal requirements as well as the requirements of our supervisors; and unfortunately, sometimes, meeting the requirements of higher-ups is a priority. Placing families at the center—by valuing parents' input regardless of their racial, ethnic, and linguistic background—will help create authentic change. Both educators and parents are experts;, educators understand evidence-based practices and strategies, but parents are primary caregivers who know their child's behaviors and potential. As previously mentioned, when working with parents, we have to learn to find a middle ground.

In one occurrence, I became increasingly frustrated with one of my student's parents because she continuously and prematurely rewarded her child so his behaviors could improve but as soon as he received an incentive, his behavior would decline. One time, he received a new phone after displaying poor behavior for consecutive weeks. As a result, I finally reached out to his mother to see if we could somehow meet in the middle. She explained to me that his grandfather gifted her son the phone, and she did not want to keep the gift from him, but she would talk to him when he returned from school and if his behavior did not improve for the remainder of the week, she would take away the phone. Although I was not in favor of the parent's decision, she considered my point of view and we came to an understanding. She kept her side of the deal, and took away the phone, and I kept her in the loop on her son's improvements. Eventually, the student started to display more positive behaviors.

As previously stated, building relationships with families is not a simple process; it requires educators to self-reflect and to respect others' differences. Cultural reciprocity is a way to successfully build relationships with RELD parents of students in special education. Nevertheless, while engaging in culturally reciprocal strategies, it is important for educators to attain and maintain boundaries during the duration of their careers to prevent burnout as well as protect their mental and emotional health. Educators should communicate and collaborate with parents for the betterment of the child, but it is important to not blur the lines between the parent and teacher roles. Educators tend to wear many hats in schools, including roles of parent, advocate, doctor, lawyer, counselor, and so forth, so sometimes we stretch ourselves too thin in thinking we can do it all. The top boundary that should be in place is hours of availability; having a set time frame where you can be contacted is vital in maintaining good mental health, and it is important to remain rigid with your set office hours. I have experienced parents calling me 6 a.m. to cry and vent about their child's behavior outside of school. I have had parents call me at 10 p.m. to express their emotions because they were having difficulties with disciplining their child. Being an empath, I tended to all phone calls and text messages during early mornings and late nights, but I had to learn to disconnect myself from the dilemmas parents endured outside of the school. I had learned to listen and provide my suggestions, but not carry the parent's emotions with me. If I had set boundaries at the beginning of the school year, I would have not ended up overwhelmed and burned out.

Furthermore, it is important to explain expectations to parents early on during the school year. Creating boundaries does not mean you are being insensitive to the concerns of your students' parents or that you do not truly care about your students' overall well-being; it simply means that you are human with responsibilities outside of the classroom. Also, when communicating with parents, educators must be consistent and cognizant of what and how they communicate to parents. Words can be interpreted in multiple ways, especially when the means of communication is via text or email. When keeping parents in the loop of their child's education, always lead with the positive, then share the adverse, and end the conversation with offering suggestions and reaching resolutions. In the scenario above, the educator did not offer any suggestions and only contacted the parent when their child was misbehaving. From experience I have learned that parents disconnect from schools when they receive only negative comments about their child and at times, they start to blame the school or teacher for their child's misbehaviors.

Damian passed second grade, but unfortunately, the school did not satisfy Ms. Williams's concerns, so with assistance from her parent advocate—Ms. Lisa—Ms. Williams decided to withdraw Damian from the school and enroll Damian in a new school for the next school year. After Damian's dreadful school year, Ms. Williams was a little nervous, but optimistic about the new school because her son had an IEP and his new teacher, Ms. White, introduced herself prior to the first day of school and provided Ms. Williams with her office hours and invited Ms. Williams to open house.

During open house, Ms. Williams was in awe at Ms. White's transparency and detailed expectations and plans for the school year. Ms. White provided parents with forms to fill out about their child's strengths and areas of concerns and asked the parents questions concerning their preferred method of communication as well as their expectations for the school year. At Damian's old school, Ms. Williams was too intimidated to openly speak to Mrs. Garcia, but immediately Ms. Williams felt comfortable sharing the issues she had at Damian's former school. Ms. White ensured Ms. Williams that her concerns have been heard and helped Ms. Williams set up Dojo on her phone so she could see how Damian is performing daily.

Educators working in high-needs schools have to focus on building successful relationships with families as well as finding the necessary resources to support their students from diverse backgrounds. Resources are not always readily available, however. As an elementary educator, I have been discouraged due to my lack of experience with dyslexia, dyscalculia (severe persistent difficulty performing arithmetical calculations),[16] and intellectual disabilities. During my third year of teaching, when I learned about dyscalculia, I had a fourth-grade student who struggled in math and constantly counted incorrectly. I kept a number line at the desk, and I had my paraprofessional routinely complete addition facts with our student, but I still felt I was not doing enough. There were days he completed his work successfully, but other days—due to his math anxiety—he would refuse to do his math work and become defiant and aggressive. I asked my ESE specialist about ways to better serve him, but she explained to me that there were not any specified services that we could provide at the school. I urged his mother to get him privately tested and told her I would see what I could find to better assist him. I feared that math would taunt him in middle school because as an educator, I lacked the sufficient skills to place the student at ease with math. The only resolution I reached was repetition and teaching the importance of mindset shift (change words, change mindset); while he improved in addition facts, he still was not confident and did not reach grade-level standards for math. Not being able to assist my student to the fullest left me despondent and frustrated. As mentioned in Chapter 2, in many states, schools do not test for dyslexia and dyscalculia; instead students are diagnosed with specified learning disability. Therefore, parents must seek private testing, and oftentimes, in high-needs schools, RELD parents do not go outside of the school to get their child tested.

In addition, sometimes RELD students with severe ID are placed in ED classrooms, where educators are not able to sufficiently serve them. I have not instructed students with ID in my classroom during the school year, but I have worked with students with ID as a respite caregiver and summer schoolteacher. Also, I witnessed other educators "throw in the towel" on their ID student(s), and it did not sit well with me. My response to working with students with ID was the same for working with students with dyslexia and dyscalculia: repetition. There was much more that could be done, but I just did not have access to those resources. Schools do not always provide the necessary trainings for educators to better assist students who are diagnosed with dyslexia, dyscalculia, and ID. According to research on dyslexic learners in mainstream classrooms, school educators face extensive challenges in delivering quality instruction and assisting students with dyslexia to overcome their difficulties in learning.[17] Also, research shows that educators in general education have issues with not only teaching students with dyslexia, but students with ID as well. In inclusive classrooms, educators tend to lack patience with students who have ID and/or SLD related to dyslexia and dyscalculia.[18] Although federal funds such as the Race to Top and Title I grants are given to many states to support high-needs school, moneys are usually used to adopt new programs that can increase the rigor within low achieving schools as well as on trainings for new academic programs. Thus, what can educators do to better serve RELD students with dyslexia, dyscalculia, and ID?

Research reveals that 3–7% of children and adolescents are diagnosed with dyscalculia.[19] About 10% of the world's population have dyslexia: 1 out of 10 people. In 2021, the U.S. Department of Education reported that 6% of students have ID.[20] Therefore, if schools are not going to provide the necessary trainings for general and special educators to better serve RELD students with ID, dyslexia, and/or dyscalculia, educators must take matters into their own hands and complete research on students with the specified diagnosis prior to the beginning of the school year. For dyscalculia, playing math games to reinforce math addition, subtraction, and multiplication facts is always better than using worksheets. Creating visual models and using manipulatives usually help students better understand math problems. It is important for educators to make sure their students receive all possible accommodations, that is, extra time on tests, independent testing, and the like, so students are given an optimal learning experience.[21] For students with dyslexia and ID, systematic instruction such as structured literacy instruction is an excellent way to teach students reading skills. Structured literacy instruction focuses on phonology, sound-symbol association, syllable instruction, morphology, syntax, and semantics.[22] Also, as mentioned in Chapter 2, visuals, color contrast, and font can better assist students with dyslexia and ID. I learned to better help individuals with ID by talking to adults with ID. One of my colleagues diagnosed with ID and dyslexia explained to me that throughout her college career, she had to teach her professors cognitive strategies to better assist her. When a child is old enough to understand their diagnosis, it does not hurt to ask the student how you, the educator, can better serve them. As always, while learning to service children with SLD and ID, it is important to keep parents abreast and share methods so they can better assist their child at home.

Working in high-needs schools can be cumbersome, but preparing in advance can ease the minds of many educators as well as parents. Lack of resources should not deter any educators from reaching their students with special needs. With patience and a positive outlook, progress can be made. Luckily, I was able to speak with my former student with dyscalculia three years later (seventh grade), and I asked him how he felt about math;

it was not so bad, he explained,, and he did not become upset anymore. While I did not achieve the outcome I desired, I was glad to know that he was doing much better. Effort from all parties involved in a child's education can help improve their academic experiences as well as their overall mindset toward school.

New school, new teacher, and an evolved Damian. Ms. Williams was pleased with Ms. White thus far. Damian received As and Bs on his first report card, and his negative behaviors decreased. He performed well because he finally received the accommodations he deserved—like extended time on tests—and his teacher made sure she kept Ms. Williams updated on Damian's progress as well as pitfalls. Ms. Williams has been feeling at ease now that she has Ms. White as well as Ms. Lisa in her corner. Now that she has a better understanding of her child's diagnoses and ways to improve his behavioral issues, she developed a token system for her son at home. Ms. White gives Dojo points online and Ms. Williams reinforces Dojo points at home and at the end of the week, Ms. Williams provides Damian with a tangible reward from a treasure box at home. Ms. Williams rewards Damian for completing his house chores as well as his homework, and now she finds herself less stressed and her son more compliant. Her overall environment has entirely transformed.

Racially, ethnically, and linguistically diverse families of students with varying exceptionalities have a difficult time maneuvering the education system, but with educators' assistance, families can become empowered. The best way to provide a quality education to RELD students with varying exceptionalities is by collaborating with families and getting ahead of any foreseeable predicaments. One predicament that may arise is families having difficulties advocating for their child. The following list are agencies—state by state—can better assist RELD parents of children with varying exceptionalities.

Alabama: Alabama Parent Educator Center (APEC) provides parents with training, information, and support to help them become meaningful participants in their children's lives to assist their child to become productive, well-educated citizens.[23]

Alaska: The Arc of Anchorage is a family-centered organization that supports children with varying exceptionalities
from birth throughout adult life. The organization provides
information, advocacy, and services.[24]

Arizona: Parent Support Arizona offers quality education
advocacy, resources, and support.[25]

Arkansas: Arkansas Disability Coalition is a statewide community-based organization that assists families and individuals with all kinds of disabilities.[26]

California: California Special Needs Advocacy provides advocacy services to students and their families to get the education they deserve under California and federal laws.[27]

Center for Parent Information and Resources provides
different centers in different regions within California to better assist parents with advocacy.[28]

Colorado: PEAK parent center is a parent training and information center. Offers free and low-cost services to families
of children with disabilities and self-advocates statewide.[29]

Connecticut: Connecticut Parent Advocacy Center (CPAC) edu-
cates, supports, and empowers diverse families of children
with varying exceptionalities from birth to adulthood. This
agency advocates at the federal, state, and local levels to help
diverse families receive appropriate supports and services.[30]

Delaware: Parent Information Center of Delaware Inc. is an
organization with a group of diverse professionals who help
inform and educate parents on best ways to advocate for
their child with varying exceptionalities.[31]

Florida: Family Network on Disabilities is a family-driven
grassroots organization with programs throughout Florida
that assists students with varying exceptionalities and families. There are links to different organization within the
county where parents share information with other parents
so they can become better advocates.[32]

Georgia: Parent to Parent of Georgia provides parent training
and information centers as well as an educational advocacy
portal that offers free legal services.[33]

Hawaii: Advocacy and Conflict Resolution offers links to different advocacy programs to assist parents with children

with varying exceptionalities. Provides training, legal support, and educational advocacy.[34]

Idaho: FYI Idaho is an organization focused on empowering parents with knowledge and resources so they can support their child with varying exceptionalities throughout their journey.[35]

Illinois: Illinois Council on Developmental Disabilities provides a list of advocacy organizations to better assist parents of children with varying exceptionalities.[36]

Indiana: Insource Special Education Parent supports parents of children with varying exceptionalities from low-income, Native American, and limited English speakers.[37]

Iowa: Iowa Department of Education provides different links to different agencies that work to develop and sustain effective partnerships between families, educators, and community providers to encourage success for all students with varying exceptionalities.[38]

Kansas: Kansas Parent Information Resource Center (KPIRC) encourages important family engagement during all levels of education and provides information and resources to assist parents, educators, and other organizations promote children with varying exceptionalities' educational success.[39]

Kentucky: Kentucky Special Parent Involvement Network (KY-SPIN) provides assistance for children who are impacted by a disability. The website provides information and resources for families to assist them to advocate for their child with varying exceptionalities.[40]

Louisiana: Department of Education Louisiana Believes provides resources for parents of students with disabilities such as family support agency, a guide to dyslexia, and information on 504 plans. The parent training center assists parents in navigating the education process.[41]

Maine: Maine Parent Federation is a website that provides resources such as protection and advocacy agencies and alliance organizations. Also, provides information on the Office of Civil Rights (OCR), and parent attorneys and advocates.[42]

Maryland: The Parents' Place of Maryland is a grassroots organization created by families, professionals, and community leaders to help provide resources, support, and information to parents of children with disabilities.[43]

Massachusetts: Massachusetts Advocates for Children help remove barriers to educational and life chances by advocating for students and families of children with disabilities who face barriers due to disability, race, culture, immigration status, language, and/or traumatic life experiences.[44]

Michigan: The Arc Community Advocates of Michigan provide statewide resources to connect families and children with disabilities to information and resources to help improve their child's education.[45]

Minnesota: PACER center is a statewide parent training and information center for families of children and youth with all disabilities.[46]

Mississippi: Mississippi Coalition for Citizens with Disabilities (MSCCD) is a nonprofit statewide organization that helps support families of children with disabilities to better advocate for their child.[47]

Missouri: MPACT is a statewide organization that provides trainings and advocacy for families of children with disabilities so they can enhance their children's opportunities and empower their child to reach their fullest potential.[48]

Montana: Montana Empowerment Center assists families, trains parents. develops collaboration between parents, resources, and schools as well empowers learning opportunities for students with special needs.[49]

Nebraska: Parent Training and Information is a statewide organization for families of children with special needs that assists families with advocacy and resources.[50]

Nevada: Nevada Educational Advocacy Center for Children and Youth is an agency that helps families learn to navigate and negotiate the special education process. The goal of the agency is to increase the level of cultural awareness by helping parents become well informed parent advocates.[51]

New Hampshire: New Hampshire Parent Information Center provides parents of children with disabilities with information, resources, and training to help children excel in school.[52]

New Jersey: SPAN independent 501(3) organization network empowers families as advocates and partners in improving education, health, mental health, and services outcomes for children with disabilities.[53]

New Mexico: Parents Reaching Out is an organization that supports and provides training and tools for families of children with disabilities to guide families throughout their child's early childhood, educational, and healthcare needs.[54]

New York: Advocates for Children of New York focuses on low-income families with children with disabilities. The organization help support parents in the fight for their child to receive a quality education through trainings, resources, and advocacy.[55]

North Carolina: Exceptional Children's Assistance Center (ECAC) is an organization that helps parents maneuver the special education system by providing training, resources, and advocacy.[56]

North Dakota: Pathfinder Services of North Dakota (PSND) is a nonprofit organization that focuses on assisting parents of children with special needs to better understand educational laws and systems.[57]

Ohio: Ohio Coalition for the Education of Children with Disabilities (OCECD) provides support services for parents and families of children with disabilities. The organization provides coordination efforts between parents, schools, and state support teams.[58]

Oklahoma: Oklahoma Parents Center is a statewide organization that specializes in educational support for parents of children with varying exceptionalities. This organization provides individualized assistance, trainings, information, and resources.[59]

Oregon: Oregon Department of Human Services provides connections to family support programs that can help parents advocate for their child concerning education, food, housing resources, legal support, and more.[60]

Pennsylvania: PEAL center is a statewide parent training and information organization for families who have children with special needs from birth to age 26. Also, the organization assists students with special needs to advocate for themselves.[61]

Rhode Island: Rhode Island Parent Information Network (RIPIN) is an organization to assist individuals, parents, families, and children work toward their goals for health, educational, and socioeconomic well-being by providing resources, training, support, and advocacy for families.[62]

South Carolina: Family Connection provides support for families of children with special needs to advocate for their child and offers programs and services.[63]

South Dakota: South Dakota Parent Connection is a nonprofit organization that connects families of children with special needs to information, training, and resources statewide.[64]

Tennessee: Kid Central Tennessee is a parent partnership organization that collaborates with families of children with special needs and communities across the state so parents can be more involved in their child's education. The organization provides month-to-month training and advocacy.[65]

Texas: Texas Parent to Parent is an advocacy network that trains parents to advocate for community-based issues, education, employment, housing, health, and transportation. The organization also provides advocacy training for parents and students.[66]

Utah: The Utah Parent Training and Information project provides one-on-one consultations that help parents work with their child's school to advocate for appropriate services, helps parents understand their rights and responsibilities and find resources and helps make connections with other families.[67]

Vermont: Vermont Family Network supports families of children with special needs by empowering families with advocacy workshops, information, and resources.[68]

Virginia: The Parent Educational Advocacy Training Center assists parents of children with special needs by providing services, research-based information and training, and opportunities for partnerships and advocacy for systemic improvement.[69]

Washington: The Arc Washington State provides information on advocacy, programs for parents, and resources to support families of children with special needs.[70]

West Virginia: West Virginia Advocates is a federally funded program that help individuals with varying exceptionalities to defend their rights and find legal assistance and provides self-advocacy support groups.[71]

Wisconsin: Wisconsin Family Assistance Center for Education, Training, and Support (WIFACETS) is an organization that provides training and support for families of children with special needs from underserved communities.[72]

Wyoming: Wyoming Parent Information Center help families of children with special needs find their voice and efficiently advocate as equal partners with schools.[73]

District of Columbia: Advocates for Justice and Education: The parent training and information center for the District of Columbia provides a parent-to-parent network of support, comprehensive resources, education programs, individual advocacy, and legal representation for families of children with special needs.[74]

Puerto Rico: Center for Parent Information and Resources provides resources for different regions. For Region A, Puerto Rican parents of children with special needs can receive information and research-based materials, parent training, and newsletters.[75]

A well-known African proverb said, "It takes a village to raise a child." Parents and schools must come together to groom a whole child to become a productive citizen in our society, and educators can serve as an intersection between home and school if they are armored with necessary information and resources to better assist students and families. The aforementioned suggestions are a start in a positive direction to empowering educators and RELD families of children with varying exceptionalities.

Notes

1 Individuals with Disabilities Education Act (IDEA), 20 U.S.C. §1450. (2004). https://sites.ed.gov/idea/statute-chapter-33/subchapter-iv/1450/11

2 Morin, A. *8 steps to advocating for your child at school.* Understood. https://www.understood.org/en/articles/parent-advocacy-steps

3 Coordinated Campaign for Learning Disabilities. (2023). *How parents can be advocates for their children.* Reading Rockets: Launching Young Readers. https://www.understood.org/en/articles/parent-advocacy-steps

4 Gumas, N. (2018). Socioeconomic and racial disparities in public special education: Alleviating decades of unequal enforcement of the individuals with disabilities education act in New York City. *Columbia Journal of Race and Law, 8*(2), 398–453. https://doi.org/10.7916/cjrl.v8i2.2335

5 Trainor, A.A. (2010). Diverse approaches to parent advocacy during special education home-school interactions: Identification and use of cultural and social capital. *Remedial and Special Education, 31*(1), 34–47. https://doi.org/10.1177/0741932508324401

6 Trainor, A.A. (2010). Diverse approaches to parent advocacy during special education home-school interactions: Identification and use of cultural and social capital. *Remedial and Special Education, 31*(1), 34–47. https://doi.org/10.1177/0741932508324401

7 Trainor, A.A. (2010). Diverse approaches to parent advocacy during special education home-school interactions: Identification and use of cultural and social capital. *Remedial and Special Education, 31*(1), 34–47. https://doi.org/10.1177/0741932508324401

8 Clinton, M., Hawley, L., & Rispoli, K. (2018). Family background and parent-school interactions in parent involvement for at-risk preschool children with disabilities. *The Journal of Special Education, 52*(1), 34–49. https://doi.org/10.1177/0022466918757199

9 Wanat, C. (2010). Challenges balancing collaboration and independence in home-school relationships: Analysis of parents' perceptions in one district. *The School Community Journal, 20*(1), 159–186.

10 Burke, M., Rossetti, Z., Aleman-Tovar, J., Rios, K., Lee, J., Schraml-Block, K., & Rivera, J. (2020). Comparing special education experiences among Spanish-and English-speaking parents of children with disabilities. *Journal of Development and Physical Disabilities, 33*, 117–135. https://doi.org/10.1007/s10882-020-09736-y

11 Syeda, N., & Dresens, E. (2020). Are school professionals in Australian schools well-prepared to collaborate with culturally and linguistically diverse families of their students on the Austim Spectrum. *School Community Journal, 30*(2), 73–92.

12 Epstein, J.L. (1986). Parents' reactions to teacher practices of parent involvement. *The Elementary School Journal, 86*(3), 277–294. http://www.jstor.org/stable/1001545

13 Harry, B., Kalyanpur, M., & Day, M. (1999). *Building cultural reciprocity with families: Case studies in special education*. Paul H. Brooks Publishing Co.

14 Kalyanpur, M., & Harry, B. (2012). *Cultural reciprocity in special education: Building family-professional relationships*. Paul H. Brooks Publishing Co.

15 Kalyanpur, M., & Harry, B. (2012). *Cultural reciprocity in special education: Building family-professional relationships*. Paul H. Brooks Publishing Co.

16 Haberstroh, S., & Schulte-Körne. (2019). The diagnosis and treatment of dyscalculia. *National Library of Medicine: National Center of Biotechnology Information, 116*(7), 107–114. https://doi.org/10.3238/arztebl.2019.0107

17 Tam, I.O.L., & Leung, C. (2019). Evaluation of the effectiveness of a literacy intervention programme on enhancing learning outcomes for secondary students with dyslexia in Hong Kong. *Dyslexia, May*, 1–22. https://doi.org/10.1080/13603116.2012.693399

18 Thwala, S.K., Ugwuanyi, C.S., Okeke, C.I.O., & Gama, N.N. (2020). Teachers' experiences with dyslexic learners in mainstream classrooms: Implications for teacher education. *International Journal of High Education, 9*(6), 34–43. https://doi.org/10.5430/ijhe.v9n6p34

19 Thwala, S.K., Ugwuanyi, C.S., Okeke, C.I.O., & Gama, N.N. (2020). Teachers' experiences with dyslexic learners in mainstream classrooms: Implications for teacher education. *International Journal of High Education, 9*(6), 34–43. https://doi.org/10.5430/ijhe.v9n6p34

20 National Center for Education Statistics. (2023 May). *Annual reports and information staff: Students with disabilities*. Department of education. Retrieved from: https://nces.ed.gov/programs/coe/indicator/cgg/students-with-disabilities#:~:text=deaf%2Dblindness%20(30%20percent)%3B,multiple%20disabilities%20(15%20percent).

21 Brain Balance. (2023). 7 Practical ways parents can help a child with dyscalculia. Retrieved from: https://www.brainbalancecenters.com/blog/practical-ways-parents-can-help-child-dyscalculia

22 International Dyslexia Association. (2023). Effective reading instruction. Retrieved from: https://dyslexiaida.org/effective-reading-instruction/

23 Alabama Parent Education Center (APEC). (2002). *Supporting Alabama parents*. http://alabamaparentcenter.com

24 The Arc of Anchorage. (2023). *Services*. https://thearcofanchorage.org/services/

25 Parent Support Arizona. (2023). *Informing parents, equipping families and empowering the communities*. https://www.parentsupportarizona.com

26 Arkansas Disability Coalition. https://ardisabilitycoalition.org/about-adc/

27 California Special Needs Advocacy. (2016). http://www.caspecialneedsadvocacy.com/contact-2.php

28 Center for Parent Information & Resources. https://www.parentcenterhub.org/california/

29 PEAK Parent Center: Helping Families Helping Children. https://www.peakparent.org/families_and_self_advocates

30 Connecticut Parent Advocacy Center (CPAC): Connecticut's Resource for Children with Disabilities. https://cpacinc.org

31 Parent Information Center of Delaware Inc. (PIC). https://picofdel.org/meet-our-team/

32 Family Network on Disabilities. https://fndusa.org

33 Parent to Parent of Georgia. *Advocacy*. https://www.p2pga.org/roadmap/advocacy/education-advocacy/

34 Advocacy and Conflict Resolution. https://spinhawaii.org/Resources/advocacy.html

35 FYI Idaho. (2021). https://www.fyidaho.org

36 Illinois Council on Developmental Disabilities. *Advocacy Organizations*. https://icdd.illinois.gov/advocacy/advocacy-organizations.html

37 Insource: Special education parent support. (2023). *Find a professional*. https://insource.org/contact-us/staff-directory/#program-specialists

38 Iowa Department of Education. https://educateiowa.gov/pk-12/special-education/parent-information/family-and-educator-partnership-fep

39 Kansas Parent Information Resource Center. (2023). https://ksdetasn.org/kpirc

40 KY-SPIN. (2023). https://www.kyspin.com/parents/advocating-for-your-child/

41 Department of Education: Louisiana Believes. *Resources for parents of students with disabilities*. https://www.louisianabelieves.com/docs/default-source/students-with-disabilities/resources-for-parents-of-students-with-disabilities.pdf

42 Maine Parent Federation. https://www.mpf.org/community-resources/advocacy/

43 The Parents' Place of Maryland. https://www.ppmd.org/about-us/#:~:text=The%20Parents%27%20Place%20of%20Maryland,and%20special%20health%20care%20needs.

44 Massachusetts Advocates for Children. https://www.massadvocates.org/mission

45 The Arc Community Advocates. https://communityadvocates.org/educational-advocacy

46 Pacer center: Champions for Children with Disabilities. (2023). *Pacer facts*. https://www.pacer.org/about/PACERfacts.asp

47 Mississippi Coalition for Citizens with Disabilities. http://www.msccd.org/about/

48 MPACT. https://www.missouriparentsact.org

49 Montana Empower Center Inc. https://mtempowermentcenter.org

50 Parent Training and Information Nebraska. https://pti-nebraska.org

51 Nevada Educational Advocacy Center for Children & Youth (NEACCY). https://www.neaccy.org

52 NH Parent Information Center. https://picnh.org

53 SPAN Parent Advocacy Network. (2023). *Special education volunteer advocates (SEVA)*. https://spanadvocacy.org/programs/seva/

54 Parents reaching out. https://parentsreachingout.org

55 Advocates for Children of New York. https://www.advocatesforchildren.org/who_we_serve/students_with_disabilities

56 Exceptional children's assistance center (ECAC). https://www.ecac-parentcenter.org

57 Pathfinder Services of ND. http://www.pathfinder-nd.org/about.php

58 The Ohio Coalition for the Education of Children with Disabilities. https://www.ocecd.org/Programs.aspx

59 Oklahoma Parents Center. https://oklahomaparentscenter.org

60 Oregon Department of Human Services. https://www.oregon.gov/odhs/children-youth/pages/family-support.aspx

61 PEAL Center. https://www.pealcenter.org/families/

62 Rhode Island Parent Information Network Inc. https://www.guidestar.org/profile/05-0457336

63 Family Connection South Carolina. https://www.familyconnectionsc.org/programs/

64 South Dakota Parent Connection. https://sdparent.org/about/

65 Kid Central Tennessee. (2023). *Parent partnership Tennessee.* https://www.kidcentraltn.com/program/parent-partnership-tennessee.html

66 Texas Parent to Parent. *Advocacy network.* https://www.txp2p.org/services/advocacy-network

67 Parent Training and Information Project. https://utahparentcenter.org/projects/pti/

68 Vermont Family Network. https://www.vermontfamilynetwork.org/who-we-are/mission-and-history/

69 Parent Educational Advocacy Training Center (PEATC). https://peatc.org

70 The Arc Washington State. https://arcwa.org/parent-to-parent/

71 Olmstead Rights. *West Virginia disability resources and advocacy organizations.* https://www.olmsteadrights.org/self-helptools/advocacy-resources/item.7022-West_Virginia_Disability_Resources_and_Advocacy_Organizations

72 Wisconsin Family Assistance Center for Education, Training, and Support (WIFACETS). https://wifacets.org/resources/

73 Parent Information Center (PIC). https://www.wpic.org

74 Advocates for Justice and Education: The Parent Training and Information Center for the District of Columbia. http://www.aje-dc.org/who-we-are/#mission

75 Center for Parent Information and Resources. https://www.parentcenterhub.org/region-a/

5

The Impact Your Mindset Has on Teaching RELD Students in Special Education

It is Ms. Neal's first year in the classroom as an emotional and behavioral disorder (EBD) teacher. She has prepped for her first year and was excited to meet her students. While setting up her classroom, she interacted with a few special education and general education teachers. Teachers stopped by to offer their advice. One of the former EBD educators, Mr. Austin, told Ms. Neal not to pressure the students and give them too much work. He continued to explain that he just gave them simple worksheets to do to keep them calm. Later, a general educator, Ms. Adams, stopped by Ms. Neal's classroom to warn her about the behavioral issues she was going to encounter, and wished Ms. Neal good luck. Ms. Neal did not care for the comments made by veteran teachers, but she refused to let their comments taint her mission and vision for the school year. Ms. Neal was fresh to the classroom, but she remembered her experiences—good and bad—as a student and decided that she would use evidence-based practices to motivate her students as well as work from a holistic point of view to improve her students' behavioral and academic outcomes.

DOI: 10.4324/9781032648965-5

Research states that deficit thinking is a common way of thinking that impacts our way of being and viewing the world. When individuals behave differently from the "norm," they are automatically seen as being deprived, negative, and disadvantaged. Deficit thinking dissuades educators and administrators from recognizing the positive values of students' abilities, personalities, and actions. As mentioned in Chapter 3, deficit thinking leads to stereotyping as well as ostracizing students based on misrepresentation.[1] Moreover, educators with good intentions tend to hold lower expectations for marginalized students, and as a result of deficit perceptions, students who attend public schools tend to have negative experiences that ultimately limit their social class mobility.[2] Research reveals three frameworks that explain deficit thinking: pseudo-scientific framework, sociological-cultural framework, and socioeconomic framework.

Pseudo-scientific framework focuses on the use of a scientific approach in unethical ways to produce unreliable "accurate" evidence. Pseudo-science is grounded in the fact that researchers who examine standardized testing claim that the results from these tests are not an accurate representation of racially marginalized communities.[3] As a result of pseudo-scientific information, educators tend to unconsciously follow data from standardized testing without thinking about how the results impact their way of viewing their students. A sociological-cultural framework is the idea that a hierarchy is created in schools based on students' sociocultural differences. Research shows that educators often believe that racially marginalized students, specifically immigrant students, do not care about school while students feel that educators do not care about them, and as a result, they fail to put forth efforts.[4] In the study completed on immigrant students and educators' perceptions, educators said that the students showed they did not care about school by the way they "dressed, walked, talked and the disrespectful tone they had toward each other and adults."[5] Finally, the socioeconomic framework is rooted in the notion that social class and economic status impact the way individuals unconsciously view one another. Working- class students from low-income socioeconomic backgrounds are treated with a deficit approach and deemed incompetent. Students from poor backgrounds are viewed as less innocent and, as a result, are seen as "troublemakers."[6]

Deficit thinking is directly related to underachievement; if an educator does not believe that a student can accomplishment anything, then the student will put in less effort. Imprecise perceptions of racially marginalized students impact lesson plans for students; educators may deliver lessons for diverse students that are ineffective and insufficient.[7] For example, during my educational career as a substitute teacher for middle schools, one educator, a very sweet lady who taught sixth-grade World History, told me that her students were very low achieving and could not read, so she gave them simple worksheets and showed videos. I questioned her comment in my head but didn't think too much about it until I subbed her class for myself. When I walked into the classroom, I noticed her class was filled with English language learners (ELL) and students with IEPs and all her classes contained students who spoke Haitian creole and Spanish. The students were given reading worksheets on various civilizations in South America. I scanned the worksheet with a translator app and the students read the work fluently in their language. I then paired bilingual students with first year ELL students and gave the students the autonomy to respond to questions in Spanish or Haitian Creole, and I used my Google translator to see if they answered the question correctly. As I assumed, the students could read and comprehend; they simply did not fully understand the English language. While the students' teacher was a sweet woman who cared about her children, she displayed deficit thinking by minimizing students' ability. Likewise, students who are labeled with a disability oftentimes are seen for what they cannot do and not for what they can do, which is why I refrain from using the word "disability" because the prefix "dis" means *not*. There was one occurrence, when my school's guidance counselor was handing out character trait booklets and grabbing books for my fourth- and fifth-grade EBD students, she asked me if I wanted books on a lower level. Perplexed and admittingly agitated by her comment, I said, "No, I will take grade level books" and, frustrated, walked away. Assuming my students were below reading grade level because of their diagnosis was mindboggling. If educators want to help close the achievement gap between RELD students with varying exceptionalities and their mainstream peers, they must shift their way of thinking.

As an educator, I constantly talked to my students about the importance of having a growth mindset. Nevertheless, it is equally as critical for educators to have a growth mindset. A growth mindset is the idea that individuals' talents can be developed through hard work, effective strategies, and help from others.[8] In order for educators to foster students' motivation, they must first themselves believe in students' abilities. Many educators tend to display a fixed mindset belief, where they believe intelligence is largely unchangeable. If educators hold fixed mindset beliefs, they may put forth less effort when working with students with varying exceptionalities. Teachers who have a growth mindset tend to deliver messages about success, provide multiple opportunities for practice, positively respond to struggling students, and show students recognition.[9] Educators must understand that they can always develop their skills, seek feedback from colleagues and/or administrators, and work on areas where they may have a fixed mindset. With a growth mindset, educators can shift their entire classroom's culture, and students will become eager to learn and strive for more.[10] My first year of teaching, I had a fixed mindset when it came to teaching math. I felt that I could not teach a student who severely struggled in math because in my head, I felt that strong math skills were something "you either have or you don't." Unfortunately, my fixed mindset kept me from teaching my students the various ways to multiply and divide. As time progressed, frustration for my students and myself grew. I decided to open my mind and practice different mathematical methods for division and multiplication problems. My students started putting forth more effort. Some of my students found math to be their favorite subject, and they began to achieve proficiency on math assessments.

Ms. Neal had nine students in her class, eight boys and one girl. One of her students was in third grade, three of her students were in fourth grade, and five of her students were in fifth-grade.

Ms. Neal had to create a detailed math schedule so she could spend sufficient time teaching necessary math skills. Oftentimes, Ms. Neal fell behind her schedule because one of her students, Rebecca, consistently refused to cooperate with Ms. Neal. Rebecca was an avid reader who loved working with Ms. Neal during reading instruction, but Ms. Neal could not get Rebecca to complete her math lessons. When Rebecca tackled a math problem, she screamed, "I cannot do this!" and threw her math workbook on the floor. Although it was a struggle teaching Rebecca, Ms. Neal would not give up. Calmly, but sternly, Ms. Neal directed Rebecca to pick up her workbook; then, she held Rebecca's hands as she showed her the deep belly breathing method. After, Rebecca calmed down Ms. Neal then directed Rebecca to read the words on the "encouragement" wall. Ms. Neal pointed to the quotes as Rebecca read "Mistakes are an opportunity to grow."" Sometimes you win, sometimes you learn." "Mistakes are expected, inspected, and corrected." "I can't do it...YET." "Today, I will try something new." "Practices makes progress." "I can do hard things." Ms. Neal took away the workbook and took out dry erase boards, markers, and counters to try to ease double digit multiplication problems into the math lesson. Ms. Neal knew she might not get the full 30 minutes of quality work from Rebecca—right now—but she would be grateful if she could get Rebecca to work for ten minutes with a gradual increase. Once Ms. Neal introduced the partial product method to Rebecca, she was able to get Rebecca to complete two math problems on the dry erase board.

Ms. Neal displayed a growth mindset by being patient with Rebecca and attempting different ways to unleash Rebecca's fullest potential. Ms. Neal demonstrated a growth mindset to teach students its importance. Eventually, all of her students will follow Ms. Neal's lead. Also, Ms. Neal remained calm during Rebecca's tantrum; remaining calm is important when working with students with varying exceptionalities. As mentioned in Chapter 1, many RELD students have multiple traumas, and individuals who display traumatic symptoms do not pay attention to face and words but focus on body language. If an educator demonstrates frustration through their body language (i.e., crossing their arms, putting a hand on their hip, etc.) the student will not be as responsive to the educator's directives. According to researchers, it is important for educators to pay close attention to what their body communicates to their students; it not only benefits students, but is positive for educators. Frustration creates tension in the body, which lessens if educators respond without being reactive.[11] In addition to deficit thinking, burnout can also stress the body as well as have an adverse impact on the mind. As educators work intensely toward improving their students' educational and academic outcomes, they must remember to pace themselves, take time out to relax, and not sweat the small stuff. When educators experience burnout, they may exhibit negativity and cynicism toward their job. All hope is lost and motivation declines. Educators could begin to develop foggy thinking and trouble concentrating.[12] As a first year educator, I almost ran out of gas, so I spoke with the counselor at my school. She sat me down and asked me, "If you were on a sinking boat with your kids, who do you save first?" I paused and before I could respond, she said, "Yourself. Save yourself first because if you are not functioning, how can you help anyone else?" I listened to the counselor and applied that advice to all parts of my life and started practicing self-care. The following school year, I was able to give my all to my students without becoming overwhelmed.

Educators must be aware that burnout is not equivalent to stress. With stress, educators may battle with everyday pressures, but once burnout consumes an individual, their tank empties, and surmounting obstacles become impossible. As a result, students can no longer depend on their teacher to uplift them, effectively teach them, and shift their way of thinking so they have better academic outcomes. Being mindful can alleviate stressors that can potentially lead to burnout. Mindfulness is focusing on the current moment and taking charge of your hectic mind. Learning to accept obstacles and dissatisfactions with clarity and a calm mind can improve productivity and outcomes. Also, mindfulness can help build community within the classroom. If educators model caring and prosocial behaviors and mindfully listen to students, they improve collaboration among their students. Mindfulness can help educators slow down during their busiest days; it helps for teachers to model mindfulness as well as teach mindfulness to their students. Slowing down can help deepen learning for students by pausing during class discussions and giving students a chance to think their answers through. Mindfulness can help educators better assess situations with "difficult" students. Approaching predicaments with non-judgmental awareness can help educators respond appropriately to adverse behaviors as well as find reasons as to why the student may be misbehaving. Mindfulness also contributes to positive communication with students. Being mindful allows educators to assess their own emotions and gives them a chance to be proactive with regulating their emotions.[13] Preventing burnout by being mindful can create an enjoyable learning experience for students and teachers alike.

Furthermore, pressures from the workplace can get the best of you if you allow them to and may trigger burnout. In my circumstances as a teacher, I learned to tell myself that "I am teaching because I want to, not because someone is forcing me. Therefore, I will close my door and dedicate myself to my students, not to administrators who do not know what is best for my students." Being an educator today is socially and emotionally demanding from dealing with high stakes testing to working with students with severe psychological difficulties. Educators working with RELD students with varying exceptionalities must understand that their main objective is not to please everyone, but to pave a better way for multiple marginalized students. A better way cannot be paved for these students if the educator becomes despondent. Thus, educators should strive for optimism, calm, and consciousness.

A positive shift in mindset can benefit the educator as well as their students. Students can become intrinsically motivated from witnessing an upbeat educator with a growth mindset. According to Abraham Maslow's Hierarchy of Needs, human motivation can be achieved only once basic human needs are met such as physiological needs (i.e., food, shelter, sleep, water, warmth, safety).[14] Many students from low-socioeconomic backgrounds who may come to school hungry, may suffer from homelessness, or may lack affection and love from parents. It is important for educators to consider all possible battles students may face and see where they can help fill certain basic needs gaps. Educators can assist in fulfilling students' cognitive needs only if they create an emotionally and physically safe environment where the students feel valued and respected. If an educator is not mentally motivated due to prejudging the student or being burned out, the student loses an opportunity to progress or move upward toward achieving their fullest potential. All students are like seeds, and how much they sprout depends on the nutrients and the water they receive over time.

After a couple of months, Rebecca's tantrums during math lessons decreased. Ms. Neal gradually introduced Rebecca to various math concepts and practiced multiplication fluency facts with Rebecca. When Ms. Neal sensed that Rebecca was becoming frustrated, she quickly pulled back all resources in front of Rebecca and had Rebecca repeat an affirmation like "This problem is not easy, but with practice I can make progress." Ms. Neal always paid close attention to Rebecca's body language and facial expressions, so a majority of the time, Rebecca was able to continue learning without major disruption. Ms. Neal's proactive strategies have prevented many of Rebecca's breakdowns. To continue Rebecca's academic improvement, Ms. Neal promised Rebecca a token for every 15 minutes of successfully (i.e., without meltdowns or negative self-talk) working. At the end of the week, Rebecca was able to exchange her tokens for something in the treasure box. Eventually, Ms. Neal hoped for Rebecca to move from extrinsic motivation to intrinsic motivation. She felt that the more Rebecca succeeded in completing math classwork and assessments, the more likely she was to start to enjoy math work and complete assignments without direction. Rebecca may not enjoy all aspects of math at the moment, but she enjoys completing multiplication facts since she learned some math tricks to memorize the facts. Ms. Neal's mindset aided in cultivating success in her classroom, but she wanted to assist in building all her students' intrinsic motivation so they could move to the next grade level with an optimistic attitude and without needing an extra push.

According to researchers, improving intrinsic motivation results in greater satisfaction and engagement. Intrinsic motivation depends on three factors:; mastery, autonomy, and purpose. In order for a student to meet mastery skills, they must make multiple attempts; students should learn from their mistakes and try again. Also, objectives must be clear with the result being mastery, and it is important for educators to provide clear and thorough feedback.[15] However, it is important for feedback to be constructive; it must provide students with words of positivity before they exit the lesson. Educators with a deficit mindset can discourage a student from meeting mastery because of the words they may utter like: "You never try," "You are always giving up," "I do not know why you even come to school." Sticks and stones may break one's bones, but words *do* hurt. Educators who mean well sometimes utter adverse words without thinking about the consequences of their verbal behaviors. Words can penetrate a child's brain and leave a lasting impact on their overall performance. As a second year educator, I became frustrated with the negative words my students used to communicate with each other, so I completed a "rice in jar" activity. I placed rice in three separate jars for a week in my classroom: the first jar, my students would come to class and say, "I hate you"; the second jar, my students would say, "I love you"; and the last jar they neglected and left alone. At the end of the week, the rice in the jar that my students said they hated had mold all over it. The rice that they left alone had some mold, but the rice they said they loved was left without any mold. At the end of the experiment, my students witnessed the power of words, and as an educator, I became more mindful of the words that exited my tongue.

In addition to using constructive criticism to help students develop mastery so they can become intrinsically motivated, it is also important for students to gain autonomy intrinsically. Give students the freedom to select an academic activity to complete. As math lessons progress, for example, educators can allow students to decide on which standard they prefer to work. If double digit multiplication, place value, and long division were lessons already taught, educators can give students the autonomy to choose what order and day they want to practice each activity.

Also, it is helpful for students to be given different material to complete the various activities. When an educator displays a growth mindset, they will be more willing to relinquish their control over the classroom and grant their students freedom to be in charge of their learning. Autonomy helps students to gain a deeper understanding of what they are learning. Last, building purpose is a significant piece to achieving intrinsic motivation. Students must understand why they are learning concepts and understand how the concepts they learn are beneficial. A great way to show students how what they are learning is beneficial is by applying the concepts to their everyday life.[16]

I had a student who was determined not to complete any math work. Every time he was required to complete a math assignment, he would ask, "Why must I complete this? This is pointless." This particular student said he wanted to be a lawyer, so math did not pertain to his career trajectory. I explained to the student that while he may not be completing math for his law degree, math concepts (i.e., multiplying, dividing, fractions, etc.) could be applied in his everyday life. I asked him if he wanted to buy a house one day and his response was, "Yes." I explained to him that math is required to calculate the down payment as well as the interest that is going to be required monthly. While the student never completely enjoyed math, he did complete the work without being redirected multiple times because he saw the purpose in understanding math. Educators who maintain a clear mind will be able to think on their feet and easily formulate scenarios like the above to properly help their students succeed in academia.

Oftentimes, general educators and special educators feel underprepared to work with RELD students with special needs. According to research, general educators do not receive the necessary training that focuses on the needs of students with varying exceptionalities, and special educators do not receive the necessary training to provide culturally relevant curriculum to RELD students with varying exceptionalities.[17] While educators are faced with the stressors of being underprepared, they can ease their minds and provide a safe learning environment for their students by simply maintaining a positive outlook. Being underprepared is one stressor that may lead to deficit thinking and burnout, but adverse communication experiences with other colleagues may trigger a negative mindset. It is critical for educators to not allow adverse communication with other colleagues or supervisors to impact their educational approach. According to researchers, principals set the tone for the school's culture, and when the principal displays ineffective communication and low morale, conflicts and dissatisfaction transpire. As a result of ineffective communication, educators can become stressed, depressed, and develop insomnia.

Also, research implicates low teacher morale adversely impacting educators' personalities. When working in a hostile environment, educators may find it hard to perform in the classroom. Educators have expressed a lack of zeal and motivation to teach with excitement because of the way their school operated. Some educators complained of stress and lack of sleep by just thinking about the issues at their school.[18] However, with the practice of positive thinking and mindfulness, educators can train their minds to leave the negativity outside of their classroom. From experience, an adverse work environment can decrease an educator's motivation. Although the leader at my school was positive, I found myself running into the ground due to ineffective communication with other administrators and colleagues. However, I could not allow negative words from other colleagues to affect the way I taught my students, so I began to isolate myself in my classroom. While remaining in isolation in a workplace environment is not ideal, it was important for me to finish out the school year with my students, so I developed tunnel vision to keep a positive mindset.

Our attitudes, beliefs, and perceptions about ourselves, other people, and our environment make up our mindset. If educators think about growth, purpose, and social outcomes when it comes to working with RELD students with special needs, they can shift their mindset to a more positive direction.[19] Mindset shifts are a powerful way to help students succeed—behaviorally, academically, and socially. Do not "drop the ball" on your RELD students with varying exceptionalities by underperforming as an educator; it is important to understand that all students have the potential to succeed in anything they set their mind to. If educators enter the classroom with the belief that anything is possible, students will follow their lead. Do not count students out of the game before allowing them the opportunity to play. There was a time during my teaching career when a young Black American third-grade student transferred to my class from another class in the middle of the school year. Before she entered my classroom, a behavior specialist told me that the student's academic performance was very low achieving and that she could not read. I have heard adverse comments before, and as always, I rejected the negative comments and waited for the student to show me their potential. The student's IEP diagnosis was other health impaired (OHI) and oppositional defiant disorder (ODD). She was taking medication for bipolar disorder. The first day she entered my classroom, I completed informal assessments to see where she should start. As suspected, the young girl could read and she was reading fluently. As time progressed, I noticed that she developed reading difficulties only when she was suffering from mania. When she was in disharmony, she could not articulate her thoughts, she stuttered frequently, and she gave up quickly. When she was emotionally and mentally stable, my student could spell words accurately, explain the main idea of stories, and use context clues to determine unknown words. Educators should not automatically deem students inept without giving them the opportunity to illustrate their true potential.

Additionally, I worked with someone who was labeled with intellectual disabilities. She was diagnosed at a very young age, and throughout her schooling, she did not have adequate assistance for her diagnosis. Her parents, who were young Black American parents from low-socioeconomic backgrounds, did not know how to serve their child either or where to seek help. The young woman I met is now in her 30s and pursuing her PhD in higher education—without suitable support. She is achieving goals that many people did not believe she could achieve. When you as an educator hear a child is diagnosed with an ID, you automatically assume that their academic abilities are extremely limited. Students being restricted due to what is displayed in black ink on paper results in unfavorable academic outcomes.

Also, educators must realize that students who have similar diagnoses may not perform the same. There are many factors that determine students' progress and, in many instances, it starts with the mindset of the educator.

Springtime is here, and while flowers are blooming, so is Rebecca's enthusiasm toward math. Ms. Neal administered multiple math assessments, and Rebecca reached mastery on multiple math topics and mastered her multiplication facts up to nine. Using partial product (a technique to multiply two or more numbers), Rebecca can independently and successfully multiply up to three-digit-by-two-digit math problems. Once Rebecca gained fluency with her multiplication facts, division became easier for her as well. She cannot complete traditional long division problems, but when she uses area models (a rectangular diagram used for multiplication problems), she can successfully complete long division problems. Rebecca sometimes gets anxious when working on multiplying fractions, but Ms. Neal is confident that Rebecca's anxiety will decrease as she continues to practice. Throughout the school year, Ms. Neal has experienced major hurdles for multiple students, but she kept an optimistic mind and pushed through the various difficulties. Also, Rebecca seeing positive results in her academic performance boosted her intrinsic motivation. Without Ms. Neal's enthusiasm, Rebecca probably would not have reached her current level of achievement.

Evidence-based practices are useful when working with RELD students with varying exceptionalities, but they can go only so far without an open mind. To this end, educators' vigilant thinking can result in "impossible" outcomes for their students with special needs. Educating students with varying needs may be a battle, but it does not have to be a sinking ship. An uphill battle ensues with determination and hope. Ultimately, it is essential to remember that science is not the end-all, be-all. There is so much that goes unseen that scientists cannot even rationalize the thinking behind specific conclusions. Oftentimes in education, as you nurture the whole student, you must walk by faith and not by sight. According to psychiatrists and psychologists, I should not be here, writing this book without the assistance of antipsychotic drugs. Based on statistics, I could not pursue my PhD and work fulltime as a single mother without the assistance of medication. Research shows that someone diagnosed with schizoaffective disorder needs to be in the care of a sound relative in order to function in this society. As I defy all odds, I innately walk in every classroom with the same ideology for the students I teach. A diagnosis of ID, ED, autism, OHI, ODD, and/or SLD should not stop an educator from putting forth effort. All students, no matter their walk of life, deserve a quality education and oftentimes, RELD students with varying exceptionalities from low-socioeconomic backgrounds depend solely on their teacher to provide them with an ounce of hope that they have not received anywhere else. As an educator, shoot for moon, and if anything, you may land among the stars.

The year has come to an end, and Ms. Neal successfully helped her students make progress in reading and in math. Although all her students did not meet proficiency, they all made academic gains from the previous school year. Rebecca received a level 3 in reading, meeting proficiency, and a level 2 in math, but was only five points away from meeting proficiency. Ms. Neal counted all her students' academic achievements as wins even if others did not view it that way. Last school year, Rebecca refused to take the end-of-the-year standardized assessment for math, but this year with receiving accommodations such as the choice of testing independently—one-on-one with a familiar face, receiving extended time, and having access to motivational growth mindset quotes, Rebecca was able to successfully complete her math test without having overwhelming anxiety.

Ms. Neal, an EBD educator, exemplifies how all educators should approach difficult situations with unmotivated students who are experiencing academic and/or behavioral struggles. In the abovementioned scenario, Ms. Neal had only nine students with varying exceptionalities in her class; therefore, experiences of a general educator with 18–25 children may look vastly different. However, the educator's mindset should remain the same— progressive and determined. When taking baby steps to success, it is important for educators to celebrate small wins, create small goals that gradually lead into bigger ones, frequently review accomplishments, and eventually turn those baby steps into full strides. Positively shifting your mind can certainly change your life as an educator. Aim for the bulls-eye, and there is a great chance you will witness your students' fullest potential.

Notes

1 Sharma, M. (2018). Seeping deficit thinking assumptions maintain the neoliberal education agenda: Exploring three conceptual frameworks of deficit thinking in inner-city schools. *Education and Urban Society, 50*(2), 136–154. https://doi.org/10.1177/0013124516682301

2 Reay, D. (2004). Exclusivity, exclusion, and social class in urban educational markets in the UK. *Urban Education, 39*, 537–560.

3 Sharma, M. (2018). Seeping deficit thinking assumptions maintain the neoliberal education agenda: Exploring three conceptual frameworks of deficit thinking in inner-city schools. *Education and Urban Society, 50*(2), 136–154. https://doi.org/10.1177/0013124516682301

4 Valenzuela, A. (1999). *Subtractive schooling: U.S.-Mexican youth and the politics of caring*. Albany: State University of New York Press.

5 Valenzuela, A. (1999). *Subtractive schooling: U.S.-Mexican youth and the politics of caring*. Albany: State University of New York Press.

6 Gabb, M. (2004). Book review of Lives on the Edge: Single mothers and their children in the other America. *Educational Studies: A Journal of the American Educational Studies Association, 36*. https://doi.org/10.1207/s15326993es3602_5

7 Milner, H.R., & Smithey, M. (2003). How teacher educators created a course curriculum to challenge and enhance preservice teachers' thinking and experience with diversity. *Teaching Education, 14*, 293–305.

8 Dweck, C. (2016, January 13). What having a "Growth mindset" actually means. *Harvard Business Review*. https://hbr.org/2016/01/what-having-a-growth-mindset-actually-means

9 Kroeper, K. (2022, May 20). Identifying teaching behaviors that foster growth mindset classroom cultures: Learn more about the importance of "growth signaling" behaviors in the classroom. *American Psychological Association*. https://www.apa.org/ed/precollege/psychology-teacher-network/introductory-psychology/growth-mindset-classroom-cultures

10 Gil, C. (2016, December 21). *Teachers need a growth mindset too: Pushing our students to adopt a growth mindset is an easy call. Adopting one ourselves is harder.* Edutopia: Social & Emotional Learning (SEL). https://www.edutopia.org/article/teachers-need-growth-mindset-christina-gil/

11 Brookes Blog. (2021, November 23). 7 Things every teacher should know about the physiological impact of trauma. https://blog.brookespublishing.com/7-things-every-teacher-should-know-about-the-physiological-impact-of-trauma/

12 Robinson, B.E. (2020, August 3). This one hidden habit protects you from burnout. *Psychology Today.* https://www.psychologytoday.com/us/blog/the-right-mindset/202008/one-hidden-habit-protects-you-burnout#:~:text=Mental%20and%20physical%20fatigue%20and,Foggy%20thinking%20and%20trouble%20concentrating

13 Jennings, P. (2015, March 30). Seven ways mindfulness can help teachers. *Greater Good Magazine.* https://greatergood.berkeley.edu/article/item/seven_ways_mindfulness_can_help_teachers

14 Open Oregon Educational Resources. *Theory of Human Motivation.* Educational Learning Theories. https://openoregon.pressbooks.pub/educationallearningtheories3rd/chapter/chapter-11-theory-of-human-motivation-2/

15 Beachboard, C. (2020, April 3). *Help students build intrinsic motivation: By fostering students' sense of mastery, autonomy, and purpose, teachers can boost their desire and dedication to learn.* Edutopia. https://www.edutopia.org/article/help-students-build-intrinsic-motivation/

16 Beachboard, C. (2020, April 3). *Help students build intrinsic motivation: By fostering students' sense of mastery, autonomy, and purpose, teachers can boost their desire and dedication to learn.* Edutopia. https://www.edutopia.org/article/help-students-build-intrinsic-motivation/

17 Osipova, A.V., & Lao, R.S. (2022). Breaking the cycle of failure for culturally and linguistically diverse learners with exceptional needs: Recommendations for improvement of teacher preparation programs. *Educational Research and Development Journal, 25*(1), 1–25. https://files.eric.ed.gov/fulltext/EJ1360921.pdf

18 Kheswa, J.G. (2015). Exploring the impact of ineffective communication on educators' teaching performance at primary schools. *International Journal of Educational Science, 11*(3), 330–340. https://doi.org/10.1080/09751122.2015.11890405

19 Happel, L., & Hulleman, C. (2019, November 21). *Three mindset shifts that can help students succeed: Students constantly face obstacles and transitions—and their mindset influences how they respond to them.* Education. https://greatergood.berkeley.edu/article/item/three_mindset_shifts_that_can_help_students_succeed

Summary

Throughout this book, high-incidence disabilities have been explained. Additionally, laws and cases were presented to show how rulings and enactments adversely impact RELD students with varying exceptionalities. Moreover, educational policies were dissected to reveal how implementation of these policies resulted in more strenuous testing and overly audacious expectations. This book showed how RELD students with special needs who come from low- socioeconomic backgrounds are the ones who are severely impacted by the many laws and policies that are meant to aid in closing the academic achievement gap between disadvantaged RELD students and their privileged mainstream peers. In subsequent chapters, remedies for the issues that educators and RELD students with special needs face were presented: educators can implement culturally sustaining pedagogies such as hip-hop pedagogy and translanguaging.

Furthermore, the importance of parental advocacy was discussed and resolutions for educators to support RELD parents of children with varying exceptionalities were presented so they can better advocate for their child. The impact of using culturally reciprocal strategies to improve parental participation was disclosed. A list of parent advocacy agencies and parent support organization was provided for all 50 states and territories. Finally, an explanation of deficit thinking and the damage it can have on students' educational experiences was discussed.

DOI: 10.4324/9781032648965-6

However, students and educators alike can have a positive educational experience if they both display a growth mindset.

This book presented multiple fictitious scenarios based on real-life events to provide transparency for readers as well as provide personal experiences to affirm best methods to support RELD students with special needs. There is not a one-size-fits-all for students with varying needs; when working with multiple marginalized groups, it is always important to keep one's culture in mind. Many educational books discuss evidence-based strategies to effectively teach children with varying needs but leave out essential details when it concerns teaching the whole child—spiritual, mental, physical, cognitive, academic, and emotional. One of the major keys to educating the whole child is self-awareness (i.e., being aware of one's biases, areas where one's mindset may be fixed, etc.). When one is self-aware, one is able to objectively approach problematic situations without blaming the child and their family for their adverse experiences and outcomes. Education is a rewarding career, but in order to reap the benefits of being an educator, you must water yourself before watering students and as you blossom—as an educator—with more knowledge, so will your students.

In Chapter 1, a scenario of a student named Antonio was presented with questions as follow: Does Ms. Blaire see only Antonio's shortcomings? What could Ms. Blaire do differently to address the issues during reading? Why did Antonio walk out of the cafeteria? Ms. Blaire is an excellent educator but has deficiencies when it comes to working with students with severe emotional disorders. Antonio could need more support or a different classroom setting (i.e., a smaller setting) or Ms. Blaire could take the time to get to know the parent and the student as well as implement various strategies to better assist Antonio.

Preceding the conference with Antonio's mom, Ms. Blaire discovered that Antonio was not taking medication to manage his ADHD symptoms. Immediately, Ms. Blaire became upset because she just could not understand why Antonio's mom, Nora, refused to give Antonio medication if it could assist with his hyperactivity. Ms. Blaire also learned that Nora suffered many job losses, and she blamed Nora for losing her job because she decided not to medicate her child. Nora walked away from the conference without feeling support or empathy toward her struggles with her son. During the conference, Ms. Blaire only pointed out Antonio's shortcomings. Ms. Williams, the ESE support facilitator, took a mental note of Ms. Blaire's communication approach and addressed Ms. Blaire in private so she could help remedy the issues she was facing.

Ms. Williams apologized to Ms. Blaire for her struggles and then continued to offer solutions. Ms. Williams started by addressing the fact that Ms. Nora's son does not take medication. Ms. Williams noticed that Ms. Blaire's eyes widened when the mom shared that she did not medicate her child. Ms. Williams explained to Ms. Blaire that everyone does not believe in pharmaceutical medicine due to various cultural and religious beliefs. She explained that as educators, "we may not fully understand the 'why' behind not using medication that can help their child focus, but if we get to know the parent, we can discover the 'why' and meet the parent(s) in the middle." Ms. Williams suggested that she have a private conversation with mom and segue into a conversation about Antonio's hyperactivity and make possible suggestions such as dietary recommendations or different helpful natural remedies. Ms. Williams stressed that when parents see that you empathize with them and attempt to collaborate with them, then the parent will be more willing to communicate and collaborate as well. Ms. Williams also pointed out the importance of leading and closing conversations on a positive note. Ms. Williams explained to Ms. Blaire that Antonio was a young boy who was simply misinterpreted and that his idiosyncrasies were a manifestation of his diagnoses. Ms. Blaire asked Ms. Williams how she could resolve the issues during reading block. Ms. Williams ask Ms. Blaire if she had ever completed a "get to know me" questionnaire so she could discover Antonio's likes and dislikes. Ms. Blaire explained to Ms. Williams that school had been hectic so it slipped her mind. Ms. Williams empathized and shared a questionnaire with Ms. Blaire. Ms. Williams proposed that Ms. Blaire pull Antonio for small group to touch on important standards and allow Antonio to work on an interactive reading activity on the computer while teaching the whole group.

Ms. Williams suggested that Ms. Blaire reward Antonio for following positive behaviors by allowing him to eat lunch in the classroom from time to time. After Ms. Blaire talked with Ms. Williams for an extensive period of time, she gained a new perspective and decided that she would make a stronger effort to reach Antonio by building a relationship with him as well as with his parent.

In the abovementioned scenario, Ms. Blaire had a difficult time identifying Antonio's positive qualities and displayed a deficit mindset by thinking the student and the parent were the problems for his downfalls. Ms. Blaire is an example of many veteran educators who lack the patience to tolerate any form of "disrespect." As educators, it is important for to understand that students' behavior is not always personal and sometimes to solve the issue, we must identify the root of the problem by asking ourselves "why?" Once Ms. Blaire identified the "why?" she was able to meet Antonio halfway by "making a deal" with him. She could provide Antonio with tokens or tickets for every 15 minutes of displaying on-task behaviors. Also, Ms. Blaire gave Antonio seven minutes of break time for every 15 minutes he remained on task. To address the last proposed question, Antonio could have walked out of the cafeteria for myriad reasons. Many students with ADHD, ASD, anxiety disorder, post-traumatic stress disorder (PTSD), or sensory processing disorders can become overstimulated by noise, lights, crowds, smell, touch, and taste. Oftentimes, overstimulation is referred to as sensory overload, where students may go into fight, flight, or freeze mode. Individuals may feel unsafe, fearful, sweaty, shaky, and the like, and it may take 30 minutes for the symptoms to lessen. Practicing deep belly breathing, meditation, and/or hand-on-heart exercises can help improve sensory overload symptoms.[1] Antonio chose to flee from the cafeteria without a word because the noise, the crowd, and the lights were too much for his senses.

Every child has a burning light inside of them that is waiting to be radiated. It is not an easy task to break the chains that leave

RELD children with varying exceptionalities oppressed, but it is a task that is worth pursuing. A dedicated educator—both special and general educators—can see substantial improvement in their student(s) with varying exceptionalities if they apply the aforementioned strategies and tips.

Note

1 Queensland Government. *Sensory overload is real and can affect any combination of the body's five senses: Learn ways to deal with it.* https://www.health.qld.gov.au/news-events/news/sensory-overload-is-real-and-can-affect-any-combination-of-the-bodys-five-senses-learn-ways-to-deal-with-it

Glossary of Key Terms

Accountability measures   policy makers monitoring the performance and progress of students and schools at the state and district levels, which holds schools and educators responsible for students' achievement.

Autism Spectrum Disorder   developmental impairment caused by variances in the brain.

Collaboration   when members of a learning community work together for the betterment of the student.

Communication   members of a learning community exchange ideas and thoughts to enhance the educational environment for students.

Critical race theory   a set of ideas that holds racial bias is inherent in Western societies within its legal and social institutions based on the idea that institutions were primarily designed for and implemented by White people.

Cultural mismatch   states that when the culture of any academic institution significantly differs from students' family or home culture, students experience struggle, which adversely impacts their academic progress.

Cultural reciprocity   the exchange of knowledge, values, and perspectives between individuals of different cultures and cultural values for the betterment of the child.

Culturally relevant pedagogy   concentrates on multiple aspects of students' achievement and upholds students' cultural identities.

Culturally sustaining pedagogy highlights equality across racial and ethnic lines and focuses on ensuring access and opportunity for all students.

Deficit mindset tendency of individuals involved in the education system to assume that when students are from disadvantaged groups or circumstances struggle in school, it is due to their circumstance, and it is their fault or their family's fault for their academic regress.

Deficit teaching approach a perspective that attributes lack of effort or academic success to the deficiency in an individual versus failure of the school system to provide an adequate education.

Disadvantaged students students who have hindrances to succeeding in school because of detrimental situations.

Disproportionality the overrepresentation or underrepresentation of a specific race or ethnicity in one or more categories, which include disability, discipline, and/or placement.

Dyscalculia math learning disability that impairs an individual's ability to learn number-related computations and concepts.

Dyslexia a neurodevelopment that impacts the way an individual reads, writes, and spells.

Early intervention identifying and evaluating—as early as possible—infants or toddlers whose healthy development has been compromised and providing suitable support and intervention.

Emotional Disturbance an inability to build and/or maintain successful interpersonal relationships with other individuals.

Executive function skills skills that refer to the capacity to plan ahead and meet goals, display self-control, follow multiple-step directions—and even when disturbed, stay focused with disruptions.

Evidence based practices practices back by extensive and quality research and used to inform instruction.

General education classroom a classroom that services 50% or more typically developed students.

Growth mindset   the idea that most abilities can be developed through dedication and persistence.

High-Incidence Disabilities   students with emotional and/or behavioral disorders, learning disabilities, and mild/intellectual disabilities.

Hip-hop pedagogy   a learning activity that utilizes hip-hop elements (i.e., DJing, break-dancing, graffiti, beatboxing, and knowledge) in formal and informal learning environments.

Holistic teaching   educators focus on emotional, social, ethical, and academic needs of students in an integrated learning format.

Individuals with Disabilities Education Act (IDEA)   a law that makes available a free appropriate public education to students with disabilities.

Intellectual Disabilities (ID)   neurodevelopment that impacts the intellectual processes, educational attainment, and the acquisition of skills needed for independent living and social functioning.

Involuntary commitment   an emergency protocol that commits, evaluates, and treats individuals who are alleged to be a danger to themselves or others due to mental illness.

Low-socioeconomic background   households that have little income to fight against adverse impacts such as health events or adult matters.

Macroculture   a dominant culture of a society (i.e., national identities such as American or European).

Marginalized   an individualized or group that is treated insignificantly within society and deemed powerless.

Microculture   the culture of a small group of human beings with a limited perspective.

Mindfulness   the state of being conscious are aware of everything around you and within.

Multiple Marginalized   a theory that states that various social, cultural, political, and economic conditions cause individuals not to be able to accomplish things.

Other Health Impairment (OHI)   having limited strength, vitality, and/or alertness to environmental stimuli within the educational environment (e.g., individuals with attention hyperactivity disorder).

Parent advocacy when a parent speaks up on behalf of their child: asking questions, raising concerns, and asking for help when necessary.

Procedural safeguards parent rights statements; if followed, the safeguards would assist in facilitating appropriate decision-making and services for children with disabilities.

Racially, Ethnically, and Linguistically Diverse (RELD) represents individuals from various racially, ethnically, and linguistically diverse backgrounds in an area.

Social emotional learning (SEL) a methodology that helps students of all ages to better comprehend their emotions, to fully feel their emotions, and demonstrate empathy for others.

Special Education the practice of educating students in a way that accommodates their individual needs and differences.

Specified learning disability (SLD) a disorder in one or more of the basic psychological processes involved in understanding or utilizing language, spoken or written, that may manifest itself in the imperfect ability to listen, think, speak, read, write, spell, or to do mathematical computations.

Structured literacy encompasses highly explicit and systematic teaching for all components of literacy.

Supplementary aids supports to enable students with disabilities to be educated with nondisabled peers to the maximum extent appropriate in the least restrictive environment.

Systematic instruction a carefully planned sequence for instruction.

Test bias when scores on a test tend to systematically over- or underestimate the true ability of individuals specifically concerning members of a specific group.

Translanguaging the ability to move fluidly between languages, a pedagogical approach to teaching.

Trauma the impact that emotional challenges due to distressing events can have on individuals.

Varying exceptionalities individuals who are diagnosed with language impairment, specific learning disabilities, are educable mentally handicapped, emotionally handicapped, or have other health impairments that require academic and/or behavioral supports.

Zero-tolerance policy   a policy of giving the most severe punishment possible to every person who commits a crime or breaks a rule.

For Product Safety Concerns and Information please contact our EU
representative GPSR@taylorandfrancis.com
Taylor & Francis Verlag GmbH, Kaufingerstraße 24, 80331 München, Germany

www.ingramcontent.com/pod-product-compliance
Ingram Content Group UK Ltd.
Pitfield, Milton Keynes, MK11 3LW, UK
UKHW021436080625
459435UK00011B/279